W9-ASL-207

Designing Effective Instructional Tasks for Physical Education and Sports

DISCARDED

David C. Griffey, PhD

Lynn Dale Housner, PhD

Human Kinetics

Diane M. Halle Library
ENDICOTT COLLEGE
Beverly, MA 01915

Library of Congress Cataloging-in-Publication Data

Griffey, David C. (David Charles)
  Designing effective instructional tasks for physical education and sports / David C. Griffey and Lynn Dale Housner.
      p. cm.
  Includes bibliographical references and index.
  ISBN-13: 978-0-7360-4175-1 (soft cover)
  ISBN-10: 0-7360-4175-3 (soft cover)
  1. Physical education and training--Study and teaching--United States. I. Housner, Lynn Dale. II. Title.

  GV365.G75 2007
  613.7071--dc22

                                        2006037751

ISBN-10: 0-7360-4175-3
ISBN-13: 978-0-7360-4175-1

Copyright © 2007 by David C. Griffey and Lynn Dale Housner

All rights reserved. Except for use in a review, the reproduction or utilization of this work in any form or by any electronic, mechanical, or other means, now known or hereafter invented, including xerography, photocopying, and recording, and in any information storage and retrieval system, is forbidden without the written permission of the publisher.

The Web addresses cited in this text were current as of October 2006, unless otherwise noted.

Acquisitions Editor: Scott Wikgren; **Managing Editor:** Kathleen Bernard; **Assistant Editor:** Martha Gullo; **Copyeditor:** Jan Feeney; **Proofreader:** Anne Rogers; **Indexer:** Betty Frizzell; **Permission Manager:** Dalene Reeder; **Graphic Designer:** Nancy Rasmus; **Graphic Artist:** Denise Lowry; **Photo Manager:** Laura Fitch; **Cover Designer:** Keith Blomberg; **Photographer (cover):** Human Kinetics; **Photographer (interior):** ©Human Kinetics; **Art Manager:** Kelly Hendren; **Illustrator:** Kelly Hendren; **Printer:** United Graphics

Printed in the United States of America   10   9   8   7   6   5   4   3   2   1

Human Kinetics
Web site: www.HumanKinetics.com

United States: Human Kinetics, P.O. Box 5076, Champaign, IL 61825-5076
800-747-4457
e-mail: humank@hkusa.com

Canada: Human Kinetics, 475 Devonshire Road Unit 100, Windsor, ON N8Y 2L5
800-465-7301 (in Canada only)
e-mail: orders@hkcanada.com

Europe: Human Kinetics, 107 Bradford Road, Stanningley,
Leeds LS28 6AT, United Kingdom
+44 (0) 113 255 5665
e-mail: hk@hkeurope.com

Australia: Human Kinetics, 57A Price Avenue, Lower Mitcham, South Australia 5062
08 8372 0999
e-mail: liaw@hkaustralia.com

New Zealand: Human Kinetics, Division of Sports Distributors NZ Ltd.
P.O. Box 300 226 Albany, North Shore City, Auckland
0064 9 448 1207
e-mail: info@humankinetics.co.nz

Contents

Preface   v

Acknowledgments   vii

1   **Analyze the Skill You Are Teaching**   **1**

2   **Structure Tasks to Promote Success**   **29**

3   **Design Tasks That Are Fun,
    Engaging, and Safe**   **59**

4   **Design Tasks That Stimulate
    Cognitive Engagement**   **75**

5   **Assess Students' Learning as
    Part of the Task**   **105**

References   123

Index   131

About the Authors   135

Preface

Although classroom researchers have recognized the importance of academic tasks in understanding how classrooms operate, attention to the structure of tasks in sport and physical education and how students interact with tasks as they do academic work in physical education has been limited. Teachers are often inexplicit in setting tasks for students, and students often modify tasks on their own. Also, teachers who hold students accountable for task performance, provide individualized tasks, and actively monitor task engagement facilitate the effectiveness of task performance by improving students' response rates (Tousignant & Siedentop, 1983).

Students are more likely to learn motor skills when engaged in successful practice opportunities appropriate to the objective of the lesson (Rink, 1996). While the research on students' engagement has provided important guidelines regarding practice conditions, it provides little information about how task structures engender high interest, engagement, and success among students. That is, what types of tasks facilitate students' motor skill acquisition while attracting students to become engaged? Unfortunately, many of the tasks or instructional activities that physical educators select for the practice of motor skills, though perceived to be important vehicles for learning, may be uninteresting to students.

Research by Chen, Darst, and Pangrazi (2001) indicates that there are five major dimensions of situational interest that can influence the appeal of learning tasks to students: novelty (i.e., new or fresh tasks), challenge (i.e., complex or demanding tasks), attention demand (i.e., tasks that grab or demand attention), instant enjoyment (i.e., appealing or exciting tasks), and exploration intention (i.e., tasks that stimulate analysis, inquiry, or discovery). *Designing Effective Instructional Tasks for Physical Education and Sports* provides the teacher educator, prospective teacher, practicing physical education teacher, and coach with several principles of task structure design. Using these principles, teachers will be able to provide students with learning activities that promote interest, engagement, and success during acquisition of motor skills. Please note that we use the word *teacher* generically and also view coaches as teachers. Examples of strategies for the delivery of engaging instructional content in the gymnasium and on the playing field are provided and should be useful for physical education teachers and coaches alike.

Before reading the book, you should consider two caveats. First, we need to highlight the difference between skills and tasks. Skills are the motor, fitness, cognitive, or social outcomes that are the goal or objective of instruction. For example, successfully demonstrating the overhand serve in volleyball (motor), improving on the sit-and-reach test (fitness), identifying the critical elements of the sole-of-the-foot trap (cognitive), and providing encouragement to a teammate (social) are all worthwhile skills or outcomes that a quality physical education or athletic program might address. A task, on the other hand, is the actual instructional activity or experience that is used in teaching the skill. For example, a motor skill objective might be to strike a tennis ball with a forehand stroke, whereas a task used in teaching this skill might be to drop and hit a tennis ball to a backboard one trial at a time, repetitively hit a tennis ball against a rebound board, strike tennis balls tossed across a net by a teacher or partner, or strike the tennis ball back and forth across the net with a partner. For achieving the skill of cooperation, a teacher could place students in partners to distribute and retrieve equipment; set up instructional tasks so that students will work together in small groups; or use teaching methods, such as reciprocal style, in which students work together cooperatively to be successful. Many types of tasks can be used for teaching skills in the psychomotor, fitness, knowledge, and social domains. Although skills can be acquired in all of these domains, this book focuses primarily on the acquisition of motor skills. Fitness, knowledge and thinking, and social responsibility skills are addressed in this book, but as secondary objectives or goals that can be achieved at the same time as motor skills are being taught.

This text also is about the structure of instructional tasks. We allude to management tasks where they are directly related to instructional tasks. However, many different management systems and methods for organizing students and tasks are beyond the scope of this text. We allude to task accountability as a way of keeping students on task and engaged via assessment strategies, but we do not address the wide variety of management strategies available to teachers (Hastie & Martin, 2006).

The task design principles in this text will provide the teacher or coach with the knowledge to structure tasks that will enable students and student-athletes to be successful, interested, and cognitively engaged learners. This will facilitate students' mindful engagement and the effective achievement of skill in physical education and sport.

Acknowledgments

When we first began our collaboration, some 25 years ago, we were both consumed with understanding what made effective teachers able to affect learning in students. We knew that not all teachers had this capacity, yet it was evident in many of those teachers we had been studying and observing. They were able to consistently help students to understand and do new and novel things. We started calling these individuals "exemplary teachers." We were each on our own journey to becoming exemplary teachers; there were many people who were generous in helping us along the path of understanding and praxis in the matter of effective teaching.

We have both been touched by outstanding teachers. Shirl Hoffman caused us to believe that there were important things to discover in the enterprise of studying the learning of human movement. Mike Sherman infected us with his enthusiasm for the study of exemplary teachers. John Nixon's encyclopedic knowledge of research on teaching and learning in movement environments set a high standard for our own academic pursuits. Lee Cronbach's continual insistence that there was always another way to look at any fact or phenomenon bred an open-mindedness in our thinking.

Patient colleagues have benefited us with their willingness to listen to, discuss, critique, and try the ideas that we were playing with. Darrel Williams's eagerness to test every empirical finding against his own extensive knowledge about helping people to learn was extremely helpful in the early stages of considering these ideas. Working with Darrel caused us to realize that many empirical findings about effective teaching and learning could not be directly employed by teachers in the gymnasium. The concepts had to be changed, smoothed, and evolved in the context of a real classroom if they were to work. He gave us daily reports for a number of years and, in that process, we realized that the language, representation, and source of empirical knowledge about teaching and learning required transformation if real teachers and coaches were to find it useful.

It is the teachers and coaches (our students and colleagues) that we have worked with over the years who have made the largest contribution to our thinking. They have constantly demanded that anything we thought we knew be subjected to interpretation and alteration by the context where they carry out their daily work—with real students in real schools and on real teams. We asked that they try these ideas in their classes and with their teams. We knew we were onto something important when they would return to us and say, "You know that stuff you taught us—I tried it, and it works!"

Because of the wonderful teachers in our lives, we are able to offer this book to you. We are confident that if you try any of ideas in this book in your work with students, you too will report back that the ideas work for helping students learn—faster and better.

There are many colleagues who have helped us—intellectually, emotionally, and pragmatically—to continue in our work over the years. We have had a lot of encouragement and are grateful for it. Chief among those who have believed in us and our work are: Mike Metzler, Bernie Oliver, Paul Schempp, and Tom Templin. There are many other individuals who have been supportive, but our studies often continued because of the support these four wonderful colleagues provided. Thank you!

Our hope is that this book results in greater numbers of exemplary teachers and coaches—those who help students learn and understand new knowledge and skill.

Analyze the Skill You Are Teaching

If students are expected to learn in a physical education or athletic context, the teacher and students need to know what they are trying to accomplish. Teachers need to understand the goal of the skill that is to be learned and how they can assist students in approaching instructional tasks designed to facilitate achievement of the goal. Instructional tasks can be multidimensional, and teachers need to be aware of the types of goals that might be achieved by instructional tasks.

For example, instructional tasks that focus on skill instruction can also reinforce key objectives in fitness, tactics and decision making, application of movement concepts and disciplinary knowledge, and achievement of personal, social, and leadership skills. NASPE standards for K-12 physical education (NASPE, 2004) and coaching education (NASPE, 2006) include these objectives and it is important that teachers consider how they can reinforce these standards while designing and teaching instructional tasks that focus on motor-skill learning.

As a result of reading this chapter and completing the learning activities, the teacher should be able to analyze the skill that they are teaching and identify the goals for sport and physical education that can be reinforced while providing skill instruction. They will be able to identify the following:

1. Various types of skills (open versus closed, outcome versus form specific)
2. Critical elements of skills (locomotor, nonlocomotor, manipulative)
3. Kinesiological concepts associated with effective skill performance
4. Thinking skills involved in learning and performing skills
5. Fitness concepts that can be taught or reinforced during skill instruction
6. Principles of social responsibility and respect that can be taught or reinforced during skill instruction
7. Instructional cues that can be used in facilitating skill, fitness, thinking, and social responsibility

---

Teaching Form and Outcome of Various Skills

Among the ways of conceptualizing skill is to do so either by the form or the outcome to be achieved, or both. The goal of form-specific skills, such as the skills in diving or gymnastics, is to move in a way consistent with a preconceived notion of proper form. All students try to move in a way that is consistent with the movement of skilled athletes in the specified sports. Outcome-specific skills, however, are judged to be effective if the student can achieve the outcome. For example, in the basketball free throw, it doesn't matter whether a player uses the two-handed underhand style made famous by Rick Barry or the standard one-handed shot used by most players. All that matters is getting the ball in the basket. The outcome is the goal.

This is an important distinction, because most teachers automatically tell students how to move even for outcome-specific skills. They provide critical elements that direct students to move in a certain way. Using the critical element approach, the teacher would give students several cues that indicate how to move. For example, the teacher might indicate that the forceful overhand throw requires standing perpendicular to the target with the throwing arm away from the target, holding the object behind the ear, stepping with the foot opposite of the throwing hand, and following through with the throwing hand across the body.

Gentile (1972) warned teachers that the critical element approach can lead to "goal confusion," in which the student tries to move like the teacher rather than focusing on achieving the outcome. Dynamical systems theorists believe that this can be counterproductive because it focuses students' attention on the movement rather than on the environment and the goal that is to be achieved. This can result in using ineffective or less-than-optimal solutions (motor patterns) to motor problems, given the highly idiosyncratic constraints and movement opportunities afforded by the interaction of the task, environment, and individual. Some have argued that focusing on how to move rather than what is to be accomplished can result in a "paralysis through analysis" as students try to move in response to an array of critical elements while ignoring the environmental stimuli that must be addressed (Gallwey, 1974).

The dynamical systems approach suggests that teachers or coaches should structure the task or goal and the environment in such a way that effective motor patterns will naturally emerge as a student solves the motor problem. Moreover, since students will bring different morphological constraints and opportunities to the problem, students are expected and encouraged to find their own solutions. According to the dynamical systems approach, the goal (intended outcome) of the task is critical because, along with constraints imposed by the individual (such as height, weight, and strength), the environment in which the task is learned or performed determines the nature of the movement patterns that can be organized to achieve the task goal. For example, if forceful overhand throwing is the desired outcome, students should be placed at challenging distances from large targets so that a forceful overhand throw is required for achieving the goal of hitting the target. Placing students too close or using targets that are too small would naturally result in students' reducing the force and increasing accuracy by using an underhand or dart-throwing form.

Using the dynamical systems approach, Davis and Burton (1991) proposed a four-step strategy to teaching motor skills: Clarify task goal by using verbal instructions or cues and structuring the environment so that students clearly understand the goal of the task, allow students to select the skill or movement form to achieve the task goal, manipulate the task (e.g., the size of the ball or height of the target) or dimensions of the performer (e.g., body position or attention focus) to assist the students in finding an optimal performance level, and direct the students in skill and movement form selection to assist the students in refining, consolidating, and extending the skilled behavior.

The approach that we adopt in this text is a hybrid approach, a combination of the dynamical systems and critical element approach. It is possible to merge these approaches by adding an open–closed skill dimension to the form–outcome dimension.

Teaching Open Versus Closed Skills

Open skills occur in unstable or unpredictable environments; therefore, it is expected that a variety of movement patterns could be used to solve motor problems. Gentile (1972) has argued that open skills, by virtue of being performed in changing environments, should be taught so that students obtain a diversified set of movement patterns that can be used in solving the array of motor problems that are encountered in open sports. This diversification of instructional experiences is thought to assist students in developing large schemas, or networks, of movement patterns that can be adapted to accommodate or solve unique motor problems. For example, when learning the forehand or backhand in tennis, students should learn to hit balls that are fast and slow, to the right and left, short and deep, and so on so that a large network of experiences are stored in memory for future use. The larger the memory network, the easier it will be for students to negotiate novel and unpredictable shots.

Closed skills, however, are performed in stable or predictable environments; because of this, more consistent form is desirable, even for outcome-specific skills. For closed skills, instructional strategies should assist students in fixating on a specific form that is successful for each student. For example, since a free throw is always performed with the same-sized ball at a standard distance from the basket, which is always a consistent diameter and set at a consistent height, whether a player is using an underhand style or a traditional style, each player would seek to use the same form (i.e., fixate) on every free throw.

In placing these dimensions together (table 1.1), a continuum progresses from form-specific (closed) skills, in which critical elements are used to assist students in moving in a specific way, to outcome-specific (open) skills, in which critical elements are provided as suggested solutions to motor problems but considerable latitude is given for idiosyncratic motor patterns that are effective in achieving the outcome.

Table 1.1   Relationship of Specific Form to Type of Movement

	Examples of skills	Bandwidth of acceptable form
Form: specific and closed	Diving and gymnastics	Very narrow. Form = outcome. Proper form is the outcome. Critical elements are taught as the template for acceptable movement patterns.
Outcome and form: specific and open	Judo	Moderately broad. Outcome is the ultimate goal, but excellent form is judged and rewarded. Critical elements are taught as a flexible template for an acceptable movement pattern.
Outcome: specific and closed	Golf	Moderately broad. Outcome is the goal, but individual and consistent form is also a goal. Critical elements are taught as a flexible template for an acceptable movement pattern.
Outcome: specific and open	Tennis	Very broad. Variations of effective form are acceptable. Critical elements are taught as a guide for effective movement patterns.

Teaching Skill Combinations

The ultimate goal of learning any skill is to use the skill in the context of a sport, dance, or physical activity. A person learns to dribble a basketball so that he can eventually play the game of basketball. A teacher should always keep this in mind while structuring learning tasks for students. Far too frequently, instructors teach skills in isolation or move students too abruptly into game situations without paying adequate attention to making the smooth transition from discrete skills to game applications. In game situations, skills are rarely performed discretely. Rather, they are performed as combinations or clusters of skills. For example, in basketball, a give-and-go can be composed of several skills. A player with the ball (the offensive player) would dribble the ball down the court quickly and then come to a quick stop. A defensive player would approach the offensive player, and when this happens the offensive player would pass the ball to a teammate. The defensive player would move to the teammate, and the first offensive player would quickly cut to the basket. The teammate would pass the ball to the first offensive player, who would catch the ball and perform either a layup or a short jump shot. The player would then block out defenders and rebound if he missed the shot.

Therefore, on the give-and-go play, there could be as many as eight skills done in a complex sequence: dribble, quick stop, pass, cut, catch, layup or jump shot, block out, and rebound, if the shot was missed. In baseball, the catch precedes and is linked to the throw. In soccer, the trap is followed by a pass, dribble, or shot.

Identifying and Teaching the Critical Elements of Fundamental Skills

Although critical elements should be used as a guide to effective movement rather than a template for all but closed, form-specific skills, teachers need to know the critical elements of motor skills so that they can use them to assist in students' learning. A classification system for conceptualizing motor skills is provided in table 1.2.

Nonlocomotor and nonmanipulative skills are balancing, or stability, skills that are performed without objects and without moving. These are basic body-management skills and are the first skills that young children would be taught. Examples of more advanced sport skills in this area are the stances of offensive or defensive lineman or the starting position of a sprinter. Locomotor and nonmanipulative skills are basic traveling skills that are performed without objects. These are also basic movement skills such as running, skipping, leaping, and hopping that would be emphasized early in the elementary curriculum before the students work with objects. Examples of sport skills in this area are running a 50-meter dash, swimming, and moving without the ball in basketball or soccer.

Manipulative skills include projections (throwing), deflections (kicking or striking), receptions (catching or trapping), and carrying objects. Deflections and receptions are both interception skills and require that the student coincide the movement of the hands, feet, or other body parts with the location of a stationary object or the path of a moving object. Projections and carrying skills are performed with the object controlled by the student. Many sport skills are combinations of fundamental skills. For example, the jump serve is a projection (ball toss), quickly followed by a run and jump, and completed with a deflection (strike) with the hand. The tennis serve is also a projection followed by a deflection.

Table 1.2   Classification for Fundamental Motor Skills

| | MANIPULATIVE SKILLS | | | |
	Projection (throwing)	Deflection (kicking or striking)	Reception (catching or trapping)	Carrying (object control)
NONMANIPULATIVE SKILLS				
Nonlocomotor skills				
Twisting, stopping	Free throw	Golf	Sole-of-foot trap in soccer	Holding or balancing an object
Turning, balancing				
Bending, landing				
Curling, swaying				
Stance in football or wrestling				
Locomotor skills				
Walking, jumping	Javelin	Jump serve in volleyball	Catching a touchdown pass	Cradling and running in lacrosse
Running, hopping				
Sliding, leaping				
Galloping, climbing				
Skipping, dodging				
Running a pass pattern in football or moving without the ball in basketball				

The critical elements associated with the advanced stages of running, jumping, throwing, catching, kicking, and striking are presented in figure 1.1. These are adapted from the Test of Gross Motor Development (Ulrich, 2000). These are only a few of the skills that an instructor might teach, and many sport-specific skills are derived from these fundamental skills.

Although the critical elements described in the advanced stage are the ultimate objective of skill instruction, the teacher needs to understand that it is natural for students to go through the various stages leading up to advanced skill performance. The job of the teacher is to structure instructional tasks and teaching strategies that assist students in moving toward more advanced levels of performance.

Learning Activity 1.1

Conduct a sport analysis. Using the classification system in table 1.2, select a sport and identify the skills that are part of the sport. Using figure 1.1, select one skill from each category and identify the critical elements for each skill.

Critical Elements for Selected Fundamental Motor Skills

Run

1. Arms move in opposition to legs; elbows bent.
2. Brief period where both feet are off the ground.
3. Narrow foot placement landing on heel or toe (i.e., not flat footed).
4. Nonsupport leg bent approximately 90 degrees (i.e., close to buttocks).

Horizontal Jump

1. Preparatory movement includes flexion of both knees with arms extended behind body.
2. Arms extend forcefully forward and upward, reaching full extension above the head.
3. Take off and land on both feet simultaneously.
4. Arms are thrust downward during landing.

Overhead Throw

1. Windup is initiated with downward movement of hand/arm.
2. Rotates hips and shoulders to a point where the nonthrowing side faces the wall.
3. Weight is transferred by stepping with the foot opposite the throwing hand.
4. Follow-through occurs beyond ball release diagonally across the body toward the nonpreferred side.

(continued)

Figure 1.1   Critical elements for the advanced stage for selected fundamental motor skills.

Reprinted, by permission, from D.A. Ulrich, 2000, *Test of gross motor development* (Austin, TX: Pro-Ed, Inc.).

Catch
1. Preparation phase where hands are in front of the body and elbows are flexed.
2. Arms extend while reaching for the ball as it arrives.
3. Ball is caught by hands only.

Kick
1. Rapid continuous approach to the ball.
2. An elongated stride or leap immediately prior to ball contact.
3. Nonkicking foot placed even with or slightly in back of the ball.
4. Kicks ball with instep of preferred foot (shoelaces) or toe.

Striking a Stationary Ball
1. Dominant hand grips bat above nondominant hand.
2. Nonpreferred side of body faces the imaginary tosser with feet parallel.
3. Hip and shoulder rotatation during swing.
4. Transfers body weight to front foot.
5. Bat contacts ball.

Figure 1.1   *(continued)*

Identifying Kinesiological Concepts

In addition to critical elements, the teacher needs to become familiar with the kinesiological concepts that underlie effective skill performance. By knowing these key kinesiological concepts, the teacher can design instruction that directs the learners' attention to these concepts. The following are several pedagogically relevant kinesiological principles that a teacher could use in teaching motor skills.

Maintaining Balance

Students can be taught that in order to maintain balance they need to widen their base of support, lower their center of gravity (CG), and keep their CG within the body. For example, in wrestling as well as most other contact sports, an opponent is more difficult to take down if he spreads the feet to shoulder width to widen the base of support and bends the knees so that the CG is lower. It is also critical that the student keep his CG within his body when doing takedowns. In wrestling and judo it is common to try to move the opponent's CG outside his body by getting him to shift his weight dramatically either forward, backward, or to the side. If this can be accomplished, the opponent will be in an unbalanced position and a takedown can be performed with greater ease than when the opponent is stable with a low CG that remains within the body.

Also, when on the mat, it is more difficult to move the wrestler in the bottom position to his back if the hands and knees are spread and a low position with a wide base of support is adopted. Interestingly, in freestyle wrestling where the wrestler on the bottom simply tries not to be turned toward his back, a position on the belly with elbows, feet, and knees dug into the mat is assumed.

Balance is important for all sports. For example, when coming to a stop in basketball, it is best to absorb force and maintain a balanced position with knees bent and feet spread with a wide base of support. Successful free throw shooting is also related to increased stability (Hudson, 1995).

Teaching that balance is important in sports will help facilitate learners' skill performance.

Efficient Locomotion

To locomote (e.g., run, skip, hop) efficiently, the student should warm up muscles to improve flexibility and fluidity of movement, bend joints and place muscles in a partial stretch so muscles are ready (e.g., in a ready position with the knees partially bent), avoid superfluous movements (e.g., side-to-side arm movements in running), have the knees high for sprinting and lower for slower (i.e., distance) running, lean forward more with higher acceleration (e.g., at the beginning of a sprint), and increase frequency or length of stride for greater speed.

Generating Force

To generate force in throwing, kicking, and jumping, the student should use summation of force by moving body parts in sequence (e.g., step, turn, throw, and follow through in throwing), run up or hop up to add momentum to the skill, transfer weight in the direction of the force (e.g., not step one way and throw or strike in another, unless this is a purposeful tactical feint), use a preparatory stretch (e.g., in throwing, striking, and kicking, as the forward step is taken, the arm, striking implement, or opposite leg is stretched in the opposite direction before moving forward to the release and follow-through), avoid extraneous motions that will detract from the forceful movements, apply force in the direction that the object is to be propelled, not stop the forceful movement prematurely, follow through, and lengthen levers (e.g., extend arms when throwing, striking, or kicking to increase the velocity of the end of the arm, bat, or leg). But the longer the lever, the harder it is to control. The student should shorten levers to decrease force and increase accuracy, as in choking up on the bat in baseball.

Improving Accuracy

Increasing force is often associated with decreasing accuracy (Magill, 2004). A speed–accuracy tradeoff is a common characteristic of skills that require both force and accuracy. To improve accuracy, the student can shorten and slow down swings, kicks, and throws to gain more time to contact the ball. Of course, depending on the goal of the skill, the teacher and student can adjust the force and accuracy balance for most skills. As a golfer approaches the green, the swing of the club uses less range of motion and force than when driving or hitting fairway shots. It is important that the teacher and student understand the speed–accuracy tradeoff and practice balancing force and accuracy in a variety of contexts. Accuracy can also be improved by applying force in the direction of the target. For striking and kicking skills it is important to focus on a contact point because this determines the direction that the object will travel. Students should also explore how the angle at which the surface is struck affects the direction that objects will travel.

Absorbing Force

To absorb force in catching, trapping, or landing, the student should spread force across a larger area to dissipate force and give with or move away from the object during contact to dissipate force.

Learning Activity 1.2

For each of the kinesiological concepts listed previously, describe two sport skills for which performance could be enhanced through application of the concept.

Identifying Thinking Skills Involved in the Skill

In recent years there has been a proliferation of research on the nature of brain development and learning (Jensen, 1998; Sprenger, 1999; Sylwester, 1995; Wolfe, 2001). For example, the brain functions by actively seeking out, attending to, and making sense of experience. Learning takes place as the brain establishes synaptic connections between neurons that represent meaningful experiences. Over time the brain builds and organizes memories as synaptic networks representing the accumulation of experience. As we learn, existing connections are strengthened, new connections are added, and faulty connections are pruned from neural networks.

In our view, students need to be active participants in their own learning. Students learn skills by relating new knowledge and skills to existing cognitive structures. Learning also takes place in social and cultural contexts; because of this, student interest, perceptions of relevance beyond the practice context, and active involvement are critical to effective task design. Bransford, Vye, Adams, and Perfetto (1989) have warned that teaching in which students are placed in the role of passive listeners without opportunities to apply knowledge can result in the development of inert knowledge; knowledge is accessible only in limited contexts, although it may be applicable to a wide variety of situations. They provide evidence indicating that knowledge can become inert if the significance or relevance of new information is not made explicit; new information is not linked with related information and applications already in memory; and opportunities to experience and generalize new knowledge across a variety of learning contexts are limited.

A prominent model that has been used to describe the types of thinking that is involved in learning and performing in sport and physical activity is information processing.

Information Processing

Information-processing models provide a framework for understanding the role of students' thinking in the learning and performance of sports and physical activities (Griffin & Placek, 2001; Housner & Griffey, 1994; Magill, 2004). According to information-processing theories, the student first formulates a clear idea about the goal of the motor skill. The student then attends selectively to the stimuli that are most relevant to performing the skill while ignoring irrelevant stimuli (e.g., internal anxiety, crowd noise) that could be distracting. The student attaches meaning to the relevant stimuli (i.e., perception) and decides on a motor response that will accomplish the goal. The student formulates a motor plan, organizes a response, and initiates the response. The student then uses available feedback to evaluate whether the goal was achieved. Then the student either modifies the next response, if the goal was not achieved, or repeats the motor skill, if the goal was achieved.

The information from these stages is available for storage in short- or long-term memory. Information stored in memory enables the student to build synaptic networks containing past stimuli, selected responses, and the success of various responses. With experience, memory structures assist the student in processing information effectively. The planning, execution, evaluation, modification of skills, and storage of information are thought to be monitored by metacognitive processes. Metacognition is viewed as the direct, conscious control of one's own cognitive processes.

The teacher needs to assist students to actively identify the processing requirements of skill acquisition as well as critical elements. Ideally, the student should analyze the skill and determine how the various components of information processing are used in skilled performance. For example, for returning a serve in racquetball, the following information processes would be involved:

1. **Identify a goal.** The goal is to intercept a legal serve before it bounces more than once and hit the ball to the front wall or ceiling without bouncing in such a way that the ball cannot be returned by the server or that moves the server from center position.

2. **Use selective attention.** The service returner needs to attend to the server's body position, the position of the racket, and the service motion. Attention to these details will provide valuable cues for labeling and "reading" the serve. The service returner, of course, also needs to attend to the velocity, trajectory, and direction of the ball.

3. **Perceive.** Based on the information gathered via selective attention, the service returner identifies the nature of the serve. Is it legal or illegal (e.g., long, short, three walls, and so on)? If it is legal, the service returner identifies the type of serve (e.g., drive, Z, lob) and, based on this information, predicts the path the ball will take.

4. **Formulate motor plan and respond.** If the serve is a fault, the service returner's response is not to respond. However, if the serve is legal, then the service returner will formulate a motor plan based on the type of serve, position of the ball, strengths of the server, and his or her own strengths. For example, if the serve is a high drive serve and comes off the center of the back wall, thereby forcing the server to

one side of the court, a good plan would be an alley pass or pinch kill away from the server for the easy point.

5. **Interpret feedback.** The service returner attends to available knowledge of results (was the response a success?) and knowledge of performance (did I move as planned?) and evaluates whether a change needs to be made in future responses to similar situations or if the level of success warrants continuation of the plan or response.

6. **Employ memory.** The service returner needs to actively store information, since what is remembered will be used in subsequent service returns as the service returner builds up a memory of past stimuli, selected responses, and levels of success. As the service returner gains knowledge, he or she will be able to process information more accurately and efficiently as the processes become more and more automatic.

7. **Use metacognition.** The service returner, with the assistance of the teacher, needs to be aware and take advantage of the information available to facilitate learning and performance. The effective service returner will be under direct, conscious control of his or her own cognitive processes, particularly early in the skill-acquisition process when cognitive involvement is high. As skills become more automatic, the returner's attention can be shifted away from specific skills to more complex aspects of the game, such as overall strategy and tactical decision making.

Tactical Thinking

To be a competent participant in sport and physical activity, it is not enough to gain proficiency in discrete skills or even combinations of skills. It is critical that the student also learn the tactical (strategic) aspects of skilled performance. For example, in basketball a student may be proficient in dribbling and ball handling, but she must also know when it is advantageous to dribble the ball down court and when it is best to pass the ball down court to begin a fast break. In soccer, a competent player will recognize when a shot on goal can be taken with a reasonable probability of success or when it is better to pass the ball out of the goal area to set up a better shot. A competent golfer will know when it is better to putt to set up an easy follow-up shot or to try to sink a putt and take a chance of significantly overshooting or undershooting the cup. A distance runner will establish a strategy (e.g., take the lead and hold it, hold back for a strong finish, draft a powerful runner) based on his knowledge of the competitors and his strengths, and then adjust the strategy as the race unfolds. Research on experts in racket sports indicates that they identify strengths and weaknesses in their opponents' games and then they attempt to exploit weaknesses and negate strengths (Davies & Housner, 2004; McPherson, 2000).

Researchers (Chi, 1981; Griffin & Placek, 2001) have argued that knowledge-based approaches to understanding tactical thinking can be used to facilitate students' use and understanding of thinking skills. Chi (1981) has provided a useful framework for conceptualizing knowledge and the cognitive processes associated with various forms of knowledge. She proposes that human memory is composed of declarative, procedural, and strategic knowledge. *Declarative* knowledge is the domain-specific, factual content residing in long-term memory. Declarative knowledge is often represented in semantic networks consisting of concepts or nodes, relations describing the nature of each node, and links representing meaningful connections between concepts. *Procedural* knowledge includes routine and adaptive cognitive-processing strategies that perform actions or operate on or in combination with declarative knowledge. Procedural knowledge is often represented as production rules or if–then statements that specify conditions (*if*) and actions (*then*) that can be initiated to achieve a particular goal. *Strategic* knowledge consists of general, heuristic strategies that are used to direct the overall operation of information processing and drive the selection and application of procedural knowledge. These include global plans or strategies of performers, such as goal setting, mnemonics, metacognition, and so on, that can be applied across a variety of subject matter domains.

These types of knowledge are important to consider when designing tasks, and teachers need to understand that all three types are important and may contribute independently to skill learning and performance (Griffin & Placek, 2001). For example, in the give-and-go strategy used in many sports, but particularly basketball, a student should be able to define the play, including positions and number of players involved, their relative locations, and any rules related to the play (declarative knowledge). They also should be able to state or diagram the if–then production rule indicating that "if" I pass the ball to my teammate and the opponent guarding me moves to my teammate to try to intercept the ball, "then" I will move toward the goal and expect an immediate return pass from my teammate (procedural). Of course, the student may be able to describe or draw the procedure, but not be able to execute the skill physically. In this case, the teacher knows that the problem is physical, not cognitive, and can proceed to rectify the execution, not the understanding, of the skill. Finally, students need to understand the overall strategy of the game and how they will approach the game (strategic knowledge). The student should understand that using constant movement, moving to open spaces, feinting to create distance from an opponent, and using tactics such as the give-and-go are part of an overall offensive strategy to get players open for unobstructed shots on goal.

The important point to remember is that when a skill is taught in isolation, the instructor jeopardizes the ecological validity of the instruction. Instructors must make certain that the tactical aspects of skill instruction are considered when they design instructional tasks. At some point in the curricular plan, a teacher needs to share with the student declarative knowledge regarding what the skill is and why it is important in the context of the actual sport or physical activity, procedural knowledge regarding how the skill is performed, and strategic knowledge about when and where the skill is used in the overall plan for the game.

All of this information is available to be processed and stored in memory as neural networks of synaptic connections. Once stored and organized in memory, this information becomes available for performing old skills and learning new skills. Learning does not happen automatically. The brain functions to actively construct meaningful representations of experience, and the teacher must assist students in using their brains. Cognitive research provides a number of guidelines that enable the physical educator to facilitate cognitive engagement and, thus, learning and performance in physical education. Educational practices that teachers can use in assisting students in becoming more "mindful movers" are presented in chapter 4.

Identifying Fitness Concepts That Will Be Reinforced

Teachers need understand that one of the ultimate goals is to engender in students a love for regular physical activity and participation patterns that include exercise in and outside of school. Regular exercise decreases cardiovascular risk factors such as obesity, hypertension, and elevated cholesterol and contributes to increases in self-esteem and feelings of well-being. Since formal physical education classes and opportunities to play sports are not always available, students need to learn to design individual health and wellness programs. This is particularly important when one considers the obesity crisis in America (Dietz, 2004).

Although fundamental and sport-specific skills are critical to students' becoming lifelong participants in sport and physical activity, one does not need to be highly skilled to benefit from a lifestyle that includes regular exercise. Fitness is an area that should be integrated throughout the physical education curriculum and sport programs. Fitness principles should constantly be revisited and reinforced when fundamental movement skills, dance, gymnastics, sport and games, or other physical activities are being taught. The goal is to enable students to play to be fit and be fit to play. That is, sport, physical activities, and fitness naturally complement one another. Children like exercise and physical activity, and teachers need to take advantage of this and incorporate fitness as part of every lesson and practice session. Using personal goals, accompanying music, fitness homework, and rewards for fitness achievement can all add to the fun of exercising and staying fit.

Students need to build a foundation of fitness that will continue into adulthood. Fitness improvments are lost when one stops exercising, so it is critical that fitness education be part of each school day. Fitness programming that is presented in short units or fitness testing once or twice a year without using the fitness data to provide ongoing fitness programming does not provide the daily exercise that students need. To be effective, fitness activities should become a regular, integrated part of the physical education curriculum, sport programs, and the students' lifestyle. In spite of the importance of fitness to health and wellness, most students receive formal physical education only once or twice a week at the elementary level and only for a single year at the high school level. This means that the family needs to become involved in the child's fitness program. Engaging in fitness activities with friends and family makes physical activity more enjoyable and encourages students to persist until they achieve gains in fitness. So, teachers need to work with parents, recreation directors, and other community resources to create opportunities for after-school, evening, and weekend physical activity. Teachers should also report (regarding the fitness levels of children) to parents and provide information regarding living a healthy lifestyle via homework, newsletters, the Internet, and the like so that ongoing participation in physical activity is encouraged.

When analyzing the skills to be taught, the teacher must determine the health-related fitness components that can be reinforced when the skill is being taught. Regular warm-ups could be designed specifically to address muscular strength or endurance, flexibility, body composition, and cardiovascular concepts that are needed for effective participation in the sports or physical activities being taught.

The teacher also needs to ensure that the tasks established for learning skills incorporate adequate levels of moderate to vigorous physical activity (MVPA). The surgeon general's report and recent research suggest that a minimum of 50% of physical education class time, including skill practice time, should be composed of MVPA (U.S. Department of Health and Human Services, 1996). In sport and physical education, teachers must remember that students are playing to be fit as well as getting fit to play. Fit performers will be better players and will more likely stay involved in physical activity after their competitive days are over. For example, a teacher could demonstrate and explain the health-related components that are required for performing a particular skill. In golf, students need to understand that improving the strength of the triceps and flexibility of the trunk and shoulder joints can contribute to a more powerful swing that takes advantage of a full range of motion. Students should also be familiar with the components of health-related fitness that are assessed with the use of Fitnessgram, and they should understand that regular involvement in fitness activities will improve their performance on the Fitnessgram.

Health-related fitness is composed of aerobic fitness, muscular strength and endurance, flexibility, and body composition. The Fitnessgram assesses these components of fitness using the Pacer test (cardiorespiratory endurance), curl-ups and push-ups (abdominal and upper-body muscular endurance), truck extension and back-saver sit-and-reach (flexibility), and percent body fat or body mass index (body composition). The Fitnessgram is a criterion-referenced test that provides students with scores that are compared to a healthy fitness zone for each fitness component. When the student is in the "zone," the software automatically provides feedback and suggestions for maintaining fitness level. If the student falls outside the "zone," suggestions for improving levels of fitness are provided. Recently, Fitnessgram added an Activitygram to obtain data about each student's involvement in regular physical activity. This was done to ensure that the ultimate goal of lifelong physical activity is not overlooked. The Physical Best program (NASPE, 2005) is the best resource for learning more about assessing and teaching health-related fitness. Following are some general ideas put forth by the Physical Best program regarding the inclusion of health-related fitness as an integral part of skill instruction in sport and physical activity.

Students should be taught principles of training that will enable them to design their own fitness programs when they are adults. For example, the *principle of overload* indicates that the body must be exercised at a level greater than that normally experienced in order to improve. If a person wants to increase aerobic fitness, the heart rate (HR) should be elevated above the level that is normal for that person. For older students (14 years and above), the level of overload or intensity needed can be calculated as a percentage of the maximum heart rate (MHR). MHR = 208 − (0.7 × age) (Tanaka, Monahan, & Seals, 2001). The percentage will vary with fitness levels; less fit people can be at 55 to 65% and highly fit people might be at 75 to 90% of MHR. For younger children, the focus is not on achieving a certain heart rate but rather on developing a positive attitude for participation in a variety of physical activities and an understanding of fitness concepts that will allow them to develop a personal exercise program in and outside of school. Children should have opportunities to engage in 60 minutes or more of health-enhancing activities each day.

The *principle of progression* indicates that the overload associated with exercise should be increased gradually. This principle emphasizes that improving fitness is an ongoing process. The *principle of regularity* reinforces this concept. Any fitness gains that are achieved through exercise are lost very quickly once exercise ends. Aerobic fitness gains can be lost within a month after exercise is stopped. The *principle of specificity* indicates that exercises are directed to specific health-related fitness areas. For example, to improve the muscular endurance of the abdominal muscles, a student would need to perform exercises using the abdominals (e.g., crunches). The last principle is *individuality*. This principle refers to the fact that all students are different in terms of their initial fitness levels, interests, and reasons for exercising. Therefore, the goals are to enable students to gain competence in a variety of activities and ultimately for them to be in a position to choose enjoyable physical activities for a lifetime of fitness.

Physical Best (NASPE, 2005) describes guidelines for implementing the five principles of training referred to as FITT. The acronym refers to frequency, intensity, time, and type. FITT provides guidelines that can be used in designing developmentally appropriate fitness programs for each type of health-related fitness: aerobic fitness, muscular strength, muscular endurance, flexibility, and body composition. The following are brief descriptions of how FITT guidelines can be applied to each of these types of health-related fitness.

Aerobic Fitness

The American College of Sports Medicine (2000) defines aerobic fitness as the "ability to perform large-muscle, dynamic, moderate- to high-intensity exercise for prolonged periods" (p. 68). Aerobic fitness is the efficient delivery of oxygen to and the removal of carbon dioxide from the muscles via the vascular system (arteries, veins, and capillaries), heart, and lungs. A focus on aerobic fitness in physical education should meet developmentally appropriate guidelines. For example, the FITT guidelines can be applied reasonably well to older students.

Frequency of exercise each week will vary according to the fitness level of a student. Low-fitness students may begin exercising 3 days a week, whereas fit students might exercise 6 or 7 days a week. Moderately fit students would exercise somewhere in between, perhaps 3 to 5 days per week. Students can determine the intensity of exercise needed for improving their aerobic fitness by calculating their target heart rate zone (THRZ), as described previously for the principle of overload (55% to 90% of MHR; MHR = 208 − [0.7 × age]).

As with frequency, intensity may vary according to the fitness level of the student. According to Physical Best (NASPE, 2005), beginning or low-fitness students would exercise at 55 to 65% of MHR, fit students could exercise at 75 to 90% of MHR, and those students at intermediate levels of fitness would be somewhere in between.

Time allocated for exercise, like frequency and intensity, will vary according to fitness level; 10 to 30 minutes of exercise for students low in fitness and 30 to 60 minutes for students with good levels of fitness are reasonable guidelines. Moderately fit students would be in between, perhaps 20 to 40 minutes. The central principle is that an exercise program for older students can be designed based on the FITT guidelines as long as attention is paid to the needs of each student. Every student will be at a different level of fitness, and each student's program should reflect those differences.

For elementary-level children, the goal should be on achieving a minimum level of 50% MVPA during physical education lessons and teaching students about the training principles, FITT guidelines, structure of the body (anatomy), functions of the body (physiology), and the benefits of regular exercise and fitness. Using HR monitors and pedometers and teaching students to monitor their own HRs and respiration rates are examples of instructional activities that can be used in educating children about fitness and how their bodies respond to exercise.

Muscular Fitness

Muscular strength is the maximal force that a muscle or group of muscles can exert in a single contraction through a full range of motion (NASPE, 2005). So, if a student can lift a 40-pound dumbbell with a biceps curl from full extension to full flexion one time and only one time, that represents the muscular strength of the biceps for this student. Muscular endurance is the ability of a muscle or muscle group to repeatedly exert force through a full range of motion. So, in this example, if a student can lift a 20-pound dumbbell for 15 repetitions before having to stop, that would be a measure of muscular endurance.

To improve muscular strength or endurance, students can apply the training principles and FITT principles through resistance exercise. Resistance exercises are designed to gradually improve muscular fitness by having students perform movements against a resistance, or weight. Resistance can be provided by a variety of sources, including training weights, rubber tubing, objects such as plastic milk jugs, or the weight of the body itself (as when doing push-ups). Children should understand that overload, progression, regularity, specificity, and individuality apply to the development of muscular strength and endurance as they do to aerobic fitness. To improve muscular fitness, children should increase resistance (overload) gradually and systematically (progression) several times each week (regularity) for the various muscle groups of the body (specificity) at a level that is appropriate for each person (individuality). Children should be provided with a variety of experiences that address the muscular fitness of the major muscle groups (legs, arms and shoulders, abdominals and lower back, upper body) so that there is a balance between the lower body and the upper body and the front and back of the body.

Physical Best FITT guidelines (NASPE, 2005) should be applied developmentally; while the recommendation for frequency is relatively stable at 2 or 3 days per week for 20 to 30 minutes each bout, intensity should begin with very light weights for young children (9 to 11 years) and can progress to more weight as students move to high school. The number of sets and repetitions also can be increased from one set of about 5 to 15 repetitions for young children and progress to three or four sets of 8 to 12 repetitions for high school students.

The primary idea is that muscular fitness is an important objective for sport and physical education, and children should be engaged in regular, varied, and individualized muscular activities that increase resistance gradually. Children should also be learning about their bodies (i.e., anatomy) and how to safely apply training principles.

Flexibility

Flexibility is the ability to move a joint through a complete range of motion (ACSM, 2000). Flexibility can be improved through the use of a variety of stretching techniques, including static stretching (stretching and holding the position for 10 to 30 seconds), done actively by the student stretching the joint, or passively, with a partner doing the stretching for the student. These types of stretching can be used at all ages. According to Physical Best (NASPE, 2005), ballistic stretching, which uses active movements to stretch muscles, can be used with older high school student-athletes, but not as part of physical education classes.

Improving flexibility by stretching is a good way of enforcing this fitness concept.

Regardless of the stretching activity, a light, whole-body aerobic warm-up should be used to increase the core temperature of the muscles and prepare them to be stretched. As with aerobic fitness, training principles (overload, progression, regularity, specificity, and individuality) and the FITT principles should be applied in improving flexibility. According to Physical Best guidelines (NASPE, 2005), students should engage frequently in stretching exercises, preferably daily but at least 3 days each week. Stretches should be done so that a tension, but not pain, is felt in the muscle. Stretching positions should be held for 10 to 30 seconds. If these principles are applied, an automatic overload and progression will be achieved, as the point at which tension is achieved will require a greater range of motion for the specific muscle being stretched.

Students need to learn proper form for active static stretching and sensitivity for a partner if passive stretching is used. There is great potential for injury when engaging in stretching exercises, and care must be taken not to involve students in stretches that place extreme pressure on the back, knees, neck, and other vulnerable joints. See the Physical Best text (NASPE, 2005) for information on contraindicated stretching exercises.

Body Composition

Body composition is typically defined as the percentage of total body weight that is composed of fat versus muscles, bone, organs, fluids, and other components that make up the entire body. For health-related fitness, the main concern is the percentage of the body that is composed of fat versus lean tissue. The primary assessments of body composition used in applied settings include skinfold measurements, which produce a measurement of percentage of body fat, or body mass index (BMI), which is a ratio of height to weight. The formula is BMI = weight in pounds ÷ [height in inches × height in inches (height squared)] × 703. (In metric, the formula is kilograms ÷ meters squared [$kg \div m^2$].) For example, if an athlete is 6 feet tall (1.8 meters) and weighs 180 pounds (81.6 kilograms), his BMI would be 180 ÷ (72 × 72) or 180 ÷ 5,184 = 0.0347 × 703 = 24.4. People with BMI scores over 25 are considered overweight, and those who have BMI scores over 30 are considered obese. Those below 25 are considered to be at healthy weights, and those with scores under 18.5 are considered underweight. So, in the example, if the athlete gained 20 pounds to weigh 200, his BMI would be 200 ÷ 5,184 (he didn't get taller) = 0.0386 × 703 = 27.12. Thus, his BMI went from a healthy 24.4 to an overweight 27.12 when he gained 20 pounds.

It is important that students understand the role of diet and exercise in body composition. In general, for each 3,500 calories (14,700 kilojoules) of food consumed beyond that burned up by daily activities, a pound of fat (0.45 kilogram) is gained. Conversely, for each 3,500 kilocalories that are burned up beyond what is consumed in food, a pound of fat is lost. So balancing exercise (which burns calories) with food consumption (which adds calories) is central to gaining and losing weight.

Interestingly, exercise burns calories not only when you are exercising but also after you stop exercising, by increasing the basal metabolic rate (BMR). Severely restricting the intake of calories will cause the BMR to decrease and the burning of calories to slow down. So, the ideal way to burn calories is to exercise and have a diet that is well balanced and healthy in terms of caloric intake, with appropriate proportions of grains, vegetables, fruits, dairy products, beans, nuts, and meats. In this way students will burn calories during and after exercise as the BMR stays increased. As lean muscle tissue increases, BMR will also increase. So, the benefits of exercise and diet multiply as a person becomes more fit.

The updated food pyramid from the U.S. Department of Agriculture (USDA), which is now called MyPyramid, recognizes the relationship between exercise and nutrition and makes recommendations for caloric intake and the types of food that should be eaten based on physical activity levels. MyPyramid can be accessed on the Internet at www.mypyramid.gov.

Learning Activity 1.3

Create a plan for integrating health-related fitness into your physical education or athletic program.

Identifying Principles of Responsibility and Respect That Will Be Reinforced

An important goal of physical education and sport is to assist students in achieving responsible behaviors such as safe practices, adherence to rules, cooperation, teamwork, ethics, respect for others, and positive social interactions. These behaviors are critical to designing and implementing an effective physical education curriculum or athletic program. Once students are able to initiate responsible behaviors on their own, they will be able to maximize personal and group success in a physical activity setting.

Physical education and sport provide ideal contexts for teaching teamwork, cooperation, fair play, and adherence to rules. In fact, Slavin (1983) developed the cooperative education model based on his observations of sport. He lamented that classroom instruction did not offer an opportunity analogous to sport for students to work together.

Hellison (1996) has provided a model that teachers can use to systematically encourage the development of personal and social responsibility in students. His model is composed of a progression of five goals, or levels. As students move to higher levels, they assume greater responsibility for their own learning, and ultimately they care more about and support the learning of fellow students. The levels are described in figure 1.2.

Hellison provides a number of strategies for teaching responsibility as an integral part of teaching instructional tasks (figure 1.3). Displaying

Hellison's Social Responsibility Model

Level 0. Irresponsibility.   Student makes excuses, blames others for own behavior, and denies personal responsibility for skills or inactivity. Student often disrupts teaching so that other students' learning is impeded.

Level I. Respect.   Student may not participate or show much improvement but is able to control behavior to the extent that he or she does not interfere with other students' right to learn and the teacher's right to teach without constant supervision. Student is expected to do the following:

a. Maintain self-control.

b. Respect everyone's right to be included.

c. Respect everyone's right for peaceful conflict resolution.

Level II. Involvement.   The student shows minimal respect for others but participates in subject matter. While supervised, the student willingly and enthusiastically plays, accepts challenges, practices skills, and engages in fitness activities. The student is expected to do the following:

a. Explore effortful participation.

b. Try new things.

c. Develop a personal definition of success.

Level III. Self-responsibility.   The student not only shows respect and participates but also can work without supervision. The student can identify his or her needs and plan and execute own physical education programs. The student is expected to do the following:

a. Demonstrate on-task independence.

b. Develop a sound knowledge base.

c. Develop, implement, and evaluate a personal plan.

Level IV. Caring.   The student, in addition to showing respect, participating, and working without supervision, is motivated to extend responsibility beyond himself or herself by cooperating, giving support, showing genuine concern, and helping others. Student is expected to do the following:

a. Develop prerequisite interpersonal skills.

b. Become sensitive and compassionate.

c. Help others without rewards.

Figure 1.2 Hellison's social responsibility model.

Adapted, by permission, from D. Hellison, 2003, Teaching personal and social responsibility. In *Student learning in physical education: Applying research to enhance instruction,* 2nd ed., edited by S. Silverman and C. Ennis (Champaign, IL: Human Kinetics), 245.

Teaching Strategies for Facilitating Personal and Social Development

Level I Strategies

1. Provide students with an option for a self-imposed time-out so that they can begin to demonstrate self-control. Students would also be responsible for deciding when to leave time-out.
2. Modify tasks so that all students are included.
3. Have class meetings to establish rules and routines that include everyone.
4. Establish a "talking bench" where students who have a conflict can go and peacefully resolve conflicts.

Level II Strategies

1. Teach by invitation so that students can begin to explore decision making.
2. Add individually programmed instruction so that students can begin to evaluate themselves.
3. Have students rate their perceptions of exertion during fitness and skill components of lessons.

Level III Strategies

1. Have students set goals for units and develop a plan to accomplish the goals.
2. Have group meetings about the contribution of physical education and physical activity to students' future health, wellness, and quality of life.
3. Have students design their own individualized fitness or skill development program.

Level IV Strategies

1. Use reciprocal teaching to encourage students to provide feedback and assist one another.
2. Use cooperative learning to place students in diverse groups in which students must help one another to achieve group goals.
3. Use adventure activities that confront students with risky activities and problem situations that can be solved.
4. Have students contract to perform service activities for the school or community, such as working as a teaching assistant in physical education classes or working in after-school or summer recreation programs.

Figure 1.3 Teaching strategies for facilitating personal and social development.

Adapted from D. Hellison, 1996, Teaching personal and social responsibility. In *Student learning in physical education: Applying research to enhance instruction*, edited by S. Silverman and C. Ennis (Champaign, IL: Human Kinetics), 269-286.

and teaching students the levels of responsibility is the first step in the process. Each day, students should be provided with feedback regarding the level that they achieved. Awareness talks at the beginning of class can be used when explaining or making students aware of the levels, and reflection time at the end of class can be used for allowing students to begin the process of self-assessment. Eventually students should learn to correctly assess their own level of performance as they achieve greater self-responsibility.

The teacher also should assist students in developing respect for individual differences and similarities. These include characteristics of culture, ethnicity, motor performance, disabilities, gender, race, and socioeconomic status. Students need to be made aware of the personal meaning that can be derived from participation in physical activity. When designed properly, physical education provides *all* students with enjoyable and challenging opportunities to learn and apply motor skills in a variety of physical activity contexts. Opportunities for individual self-expression and social interaction in groups are also provided in high-quality physical education programs. When these types of programs are made available, the benefits are obvious to students, and the students are enticed to continue participating in physical activity throughout their lifetime. Conversely, poorly constructed physical education programs can turn off students from physical education in particular and physical activity in general.

Selecting Instructional Cues That Will Be Used

Pedagogical content knowledge (PCK) has become an important theoretical and practical concept in research on teaching effectiveness. Shulman (1987) defines PCK as transforming subject matter and representing it to students in a comprehensible form. In representing content knowledge, "analogies, metaphors, examples, demonstrations, simulations, and the like can help to build a bridge between the teacher's comprehension and that desired for the students" (p. 16).

Sport and physical education are domains in which teaching is conducted through the use of rich techniques for representing knowledge to the learner (Gallwey, 1974; Torbert, 1982). One powerful form of PCK in the area of sport and physical activity is the use of instructional cues to help students focus attention on critical aspects (e.g., elements, tactics, and so on) of the skill (Fronske, 2001; Fronske & Wilson, 2002; Griffey, Housner, & Williams, 1986; Masser, 1993). Instructional cues present students with meaningful, organized "chunks" of information rather than discrete elements so that memory is facilitated. Housner and Griffey (1994) identified four types of cues that coaches and teachers use in focusing students' attention: verbal, visual, kinesthetic/tactile, and task structure cues.

Several examples are provided in the following paragraphs. A more detailed analysis of the use of instructional cues in engaging students cognitively is presented in chapter 4.

The rhyme "Ball high, fingers to the sky; ball low, fingers to the toes" is an example of a **verbal cue** because it can assist children in remembering hand positions when catching objects that are high or low. The verbal cue "put the penny in the basket" can enhance the proper follow-through in the free throw. The back-scratch position in the tennis serve provides a vivid cue for indicating the position of the racket head as the ball toss is performed. Prompting students to ask themselves, "What will I do if the ball comes to me?" can stimulate decision making before the actual event. There are hundreds of verbal cues that can assist students in learning and retaining motor skills.

Visual cues include demonstrations, videos, graphic representations, targets on objects, and other devices that assist the learner in focusing attention visually on the most relevant stimuli. Many teachers focus students' visual attention by placing visible targets or marks (e.g., Xs, faces, numbers) on objects that are to be intercepted for kicking, catching, or striking. Sometimes a verbal cue can stimulate the elicitation of a visual image that can make the movement easier to perform and remember. For example, in a soccer lesson, "Heading is like a chicken pecking. With hands in the armpits you make a pecking motion and head the ball at the hairline."

Kinesthetic/tactile cues involve the teacher's directing or guiding the learner in reproducing a particular motor pattern. Manual guidance, which involves touching or moving the learner's body parts (e.g., touching the leg that a student should step with when batting), and mechanical guidance, in which movements are directed through the use of external objects or devices (e.g., practice belts in diving or gymnastics), are two methods teachers use in assisting students in learning a motor pattern. Having students place the forward foot on a short piece of lumber (such a four-by-four board) will encourage them to shift their weight to the rear during the preparation phase of throwing and step forward (step off the four-by-four) during the throw. Placing a student with his back 2 to 3 feet (61 to 91 cm) from a wall and then instructing the child to reach back and touch the ball to the wall before throwing will encourage the student to extend the arms before throwing. Simply moving the student to the proper position can be an effective cue.

Task structure cues include any task or activity structure that focuses students cognitively during skill practice. Task structure cues are used to design the practice environment so that the attention is directed to some aspect of the skill. For example, in basketball, players can be encouraged to use a high arc in the free throw by placing a rope in front of and higher than the front of the basket. The rope provides a concrete obstacle that forces the shooter to arc the ball over the rope. Teachers place a rope a foot or so off the ground and in front of a student performing a standing broad jump, which forces the student to jump over the rope, thereby increasing the elevation and distance of the jump.

There are hundreds of cues that can assist students in learning and retaining motor skills. However, teachers need to recognize that the use of cues is not restricted to teaching the critical elements of motor skills. Teachers can also use cues to convey information regarding fitness concepts, personal and social skills, and the cognitive aspects of skill learning. For example, the cue "Move to the open space" focuses the students' attention on a strategic concept of getting open by moving to spaces unoccupied by defenders. The cue "*Slow* down, don't *sit* down" focuses on the importance of moving continuously during fitness activities and that when rest is needed, students can obtain it by slowing down instead of sitting down. Similarly, "If you can't talk, you need to walk" can assist students in understanding that exercising at a level of intensity that is too high can fatigue the students and cause them to stop exercising too soon. Finally, the cue "Don't trouble your neighbor's bubble" can remind children that they need to respect one another's personal space.

Learning Activity 1.4

Identify two instructional cues that you have found to be effective for each of the following skills: motor, thinking, fitness, and social-interaction skills.

Summary

This chapter introduces the multidimensionality of teaching physical education and athletics. When teaching skills, good teachers integrate principles of fitness, thinking skills, and positive social interaction. This chapter emphasizes the importance of identifying the various goals and objectives of physical education and athletics so that the teacher can clearly and systematically design and implement instruction. The goals and objectives included in this chapter are consistent with recent NASPE standards. Following are the six recently revised (NASPE, 2004) K-12 national standards:

Standard 1. Demonstrates competency in motor skills and movement patterns needed to perform a variety of physical activities. This standard provides competence in a foundation of many fundamental movement skills at the elementary level that can be used to facilitate the acquisition of specialized movement skills later. The successful acquisition of skills will increase the likelihood of students' participation in physical activities after school-based physical education and sport opportunities end.

Standard 2. Demonstrates understanding of movement concepts, principles, strategies, and tactics as they apply to the learning and performance of physical activities. This standard assists the learner in using cognitive skills from motor learning and development, exercise physiology, biomechanics, and so on, to enhance skill learning and performance.

Standards 3 and 4. Participates regularly in physical activity and achieves and maintains a health-enhancing level of physical fitness. Students should enjoy physical activity and participate in exercise in and outside formal school-based physical education and sport programs. It is imperative that students learn how to design their own individual program for maintaining health and wellness and understand the health benefits of regular exercise.

Standard 5. Exhibits responsible personal and social behavior that respects self and others in physical activity settings. Students need to engage in responsible behaviors such as complying with rules, exhibiting sportspersonship, cooperating with fellow students, working as a team, and showing respect for others. Students who are responsible for their own behavior will be better able to succeed in individual and group settings.

Standard 6. Values physical activity for health, enjoyment, challenge, self-expression, and/or social interaction. Students need to be personally aware of the meaning that participation in physical activity can have for them. Sport and physical education programs need to provide *all* students with enjoyable and challenging learning opportunities that encourage self-expression and social interaction. Programs designed to include these characteristics are more likely to stimulate students to value and participate in physical activity as part of their lifestyle. Poor programs, on the other hand, will contribute to poor attitudes toward physical education and physical activity.

Moving into the Future: National Standards for Physical Education, 2nd Edition (2004) reprinted with permission from the National Association for Sport and Physical Education (NASPE), 1900 Association Drive, Reston, VA 20191-1599.

Structure Tasks to Promote Success

Facilitating successful task performance is the heart of effective task design. As previously mentioned, students' time on task is necessary but insufficient for enhancing learning. It is critical for students to have moderate to high levels of success for optimal learning to take place. Academic learning time in physical education (ALT-PE) is defined as the time that students are engaged in activities related to the objectives of the lesson at moderate to high levels of success. One way to ensure that students remain engaged and interested is to design tasks that enable them to succeed (Silverman, 2005).

When designing tasks, the teacher needs to plan for students of varying ability and structure tasks that will permit students to be successful, yet challenged. Tasks that are too easy or too difficult can cause students to lose interest. As the Goldilocks principle states, tasks should not be too hard or too easy; they should be *just right.* Students need to be constantly challenged and motivated in the physical education class or sport settings. Tasks need to be matched to students' ability levels so that they can achieve a moderately high degree (approximately 70 to 80%) of success. How a teacher structures tasks will determine, to a large degree, the success that students achieve.

In this chapter a variety of strategies are presented that will assist teachers in designing and modifying tasks to increase students' success. Upon completion of this chapter, the teacher should be able to do the following:

1. Arrange tasks progressively.
2. Provide individualized instruction.
3. Make adjustments based on students' skill level.
4. Check that students are ready before playing games.
5. Modify games to make them more developmentally appropriate.
6. Apply the sport education model.

Arrange Tasks Progressively

A developmentally appropriate program of physical education or athletics focuses on the development of prerequisite motor skills before applying skills in game settings. Some physical education classes and youth sport programs place students in actual games before they are ready. When students do not have the skills to successfully play the game, frustration and off-task behavior can be the result. Students need to practice skills in a variety of nonthreatening environments that are conducive to high degrees of success and where mistakes are considered to be part of the skill-acquisition process.

Making sure that learners can practice skills in a gradual progression to game-like scenarios encourages success and enjoyment.

When students display skill competence, then a gradual progression to more game-like situations can be made. Even if a student can perform a skill in a controlled environment, it does not mean that he can apply this skill in a game situation. Placing students in game-like settings before they are ready can result in a decline in performance level and frustration. The following are several techniques that can be used in developing task progressions for various physical activity areas.

Task Analysis

Once the teacher has selected the motor skill that will be taught, the learning tasks can then be designed and organized from simple to complex. Sequencing tasks from simple to complex is quite easy through the application of a task analytic procedure (Herkowicz, 1978; Langely & Woods, 1997). In task analysis, a skill is analyzed in order to identify the many variables that can influence the way the skill can be performed. The teacher simply asks herself, "What factors make any particular motor skill easier or more difficult to perform?" This will enable the teacher to identify numerous alternatives for modifying activities, which will appropriately challenge students as they learn and refine their skills. Using the task analytic approach, a teacher is able to develop a sequence of task progressions that will enable each student to be appropriately challenged in a variety of ways. Adding new requirements for a task such as time, accuracy, or performing with other students will help the student to refine and develop skills. A simple example of this approach is provided in figure 2.1.

The movement concepts used in movement education approaches to teaching and presented in table 2.1 are extremely useful when performing task analyses. Carson (2000) describes the types of awareness (action, effort, spatial, body) that result from understanding movement concepts that can provide students with a variety of challenges when learning new skills.

- Effort awareness is *how* the body moves to start, stop, and continue a movement. Students need to be able to move at different speeds and control changes in the speed of movements. For example, when learning to dribble

Skill Progression for Kicking and Passing

The student has developed a competent kicking or passing skill using a variety of balls. Now the student needs learning tasks that will be challenging and will facilitate the transition to more complex, game-like situations.

1. Kicking or passing at different distances (short, moderate, long kicks with no accuracy)

2. Kicking or passing for accuracy (small, medium, large target areas)

3. Kicking or passing to a partner (partner is stationary and moving)

4. Kicking or passing to a partner while moving (forward, right, left)

5. Kicking or passing to a partner while being guarded by a single opponent (2 on 1)

6. Kicking or passing to two partners while being guarded by two opponents (3 on 2)

Figure 2.1 Skill progression for kicking and passing.

a soccer ball, students need to be able to walk, jog, and run while controlling the ball. Force is an element of effort. Students often focus on striking as hard as they can or throwing an object as high as they can. Practicing all of the levels of force helps students to realize that they can move forcefully or softly and gently. Creating or absorbing force allows students to see how much muscular tension is required for starting, stopping, or maintaining movements. Absorbing force is how the body parts "give," or absorb force, when catching, trapping a ball, or landing during a jump. Rhythm is an element of effort and operates when students move in response to a song, beat, or chant, or when they are controlling the pace of movements. Movements can be static (as when holding a handstand), explosive (as when striking a ball), or sustained (as when jogging). Control is the coordination of the movement. Students need to practice making transitions between combinations of movements. When movements are combined or sequenced, the continuity of the whole movement sequence often diminishes. Practice should be designed to assist the student in controlling movements both in isolation and in combinations.

• Spatial awareness is *where* the body moves. Space is divided into two categories: personal and general. Personal space (sometimes called self-space) is the space immediately surrounding a person, typically an arm's length. Personal space is used by teachers to arrange students so that no one is too close or so students can practice skills without being disturbed by others. General space (sometimes called shared space) is the space beyond personal space that is available to everyone. General space is the entire activity area (e.g., gym or field) unless the teacher establishes boundaries or rules that define the general space that is to be used. Movement occurs in various directions (forward, backward, and sideways; right and left; up and down; clockwise, counterclockwise), levels (low, medium, high), and pathways (straight, curved, zigzag, shapes). Students should be given opportunities to practice performing motor skills using these concepts, since most sports and games require the performer to move in various directions, levels, and pathways. For example, in baseball or softball, players catch balls at all levels: low (grounders), medium (line drives), and high (pop-ups). A basketball player will dribble in various pathways and directions. Good basketball players can dribble forward, backward, and sideways while traveling in straight, curved, and zigzag pathways. Also, the wide receiver in football uses a variety of pass patterns that incorporate straight, curved, and zigzag pathways. Students need to be able to locomote in a variety of ways with and without objects when using these pathways. Most coaches at all levels intuitively use task analysis to design practices because they know the complexity and variations involved in becoming a proficient athletic performer.

• Body awareness is an understanding of the *relationships* among the body parts and with other movers or objects. Body-part identification

Table 2.1 "I Am Learning" Curriculum

I am learning **what** my body does, **how** and **where** my body moves, and how **my body relates** to myself, other movers, and objects.

Action awareness: "I am learning **what** my body does."

Traveling skills	Stabilizing skills	Manipulating skills
Walking, jumping, running, hopping, sliding, leaping, galloping, climbing, skipping, crawling	Twisting, stopping, pushing, turning, balancing, pulling, bending, landing, dodging, stretching, swinging, curling, swaying	Throwing, rolling, catching, trapping, kicking, bouncing, striking, tossing, object handling

Effort awareness: "I am learning **how** my body moves."

Time		Force			Control	
Speeds	**Rhythm**	**Degrees of force**	**Creating force**	**Absorbing force**	**Weight transfer**	**Dimensions**
Slow	Beats	Strong	Starting	Stopping	Rocking	Single movements
Medium	Cadence	Medium	Sustained	Receiving		
Fast	Patterns	Light	Explosive	Stabilizing	Stepping	Combinations of rolling movements
Accelerating			Gradual	Static		
Decelerating					Flight	Transitions

Spatial awareness: "I am learning **where** my body moves."

Categories	Directions	Levels	Pathways
Self-space	Right, left	High	Straight
Shared space	Up, down	Medium	Curved
	Forward	Low	Zigzag
	Backward		Shapes
	Sideways		
	Clockwise		
	Counterclockwise		

Body awareness: "I am learning about the **relationships** my body creates."

With myself		Other movers and objects		
Body parts	**Body shapes**	**Roles**	**Locations**	
Head, arms, ankles	Big	Leading	Near to/far from	
Neck, waist, toes	Small	Following	Over/under	
Ears, chest, elbow	Curved	Mirroring	In front/behind	
Eyes, tummy, wrist	Straight	Unison	On/off	
Nose, hips, hand	Wide	Alternately	Together/apart	
Shoulder, leg, fingers	Twisted	Solo	Facing/side by side	
Knee, bottom	Like	Partner	Around/through	
Back, foot	Unlike	Group		

INTEGRATED PHYSICAL EDUCATION; GUIDE FOR ELEMENTARY CLASSROOM TEACHER by L.D. Housner. Copyright 2000 by FITNESS INFORMATION TECHNOLOGY, INC. Reproduced with permission of FITNESS INFORMATION TECHNOLOGY, INC. in the format Textbook via Copyright Clearance Center.

Movement concepts can be used in performing a task analysis of basketball dribbling. Figure 2.2 is an analysis of dribbling while stationary in personal space.

Elements	LEVELS OF DIFFICULTY		
	1	2	3
1. Different hands	Right	Left	Alternating
2. Different levels	Low (seated)	Medium (knees)	High (standing)
3. Force	Soft	Medium	Hard
4. Ball size	Large	Medium	Small
5. Rhythm	Without	With	
6. Number of dribbles	5	10	20
7. Eyes	Open	Closed*	

* Note: Use only with stationary dribble.

For this analysis, the simplest task would be dribbling a medium-sized ball 5 times with the right hand (for a right-handed student), without rhythm, with soft force, with eyes open, and while sitting (low level). The most difficult task is probably dribbling a small ball 20 times with alternating hands, to a rhythm, with strong force, with eyes closed, while standing. In between these tasks there are 970 possible tasks that can be organized from simple to complex (hands [3 levels] $\times$ levels [3 levels] $\times$ force [3 levels] $\times$ ball size [3 levels] $\times$ rhythm [2 levels]) $\times$ number [3 levels] $\times$ eyes [2 levels] = $3 \times 3 \times 3 \times 3 \times 2 \times 3 \times 2 = 972$).

Figure 2.2 An example of task analysis for basketball.

makes movement more meaningful for students (Carson, 2000). Identifying body parts and using them to balance objects help students to develop knowledge of their bodies. Exploring body shapes allows students to discover the shapes the body can and cannot make. Relationships between the mover and other movers and objects are important elements of body awareness. Roles such as leader, follower, and partner can be used in practicing relationships. The location (near to or far from, over or under, in front of or behind, on or off) of the mover relative to other people or objects is an element of body awareness. Since most team sports involve moving in general space with objects and teammates as they contend with opposing players, teachers and coaches need to structure practice tasks so that students will move toward increasing interactions between players and opponents.

Learning Activity 2.1

Create a task analysis for each of the following: fielding ground balls and throwing, doing an underhand serve in volleyball, jumping rope, and throwing passes in football. Ask yourself, "What elements will change how each task is performed?" Identify the elements that will affect the level of difficulty for performing each task, and organize the levels within each element from the simplest to the most complex.

Students are very good at task analysis and, when possible, they should be provided with opportunities to participate in the process of building and modifying task structures. Involving students will make them more active, interested, and successful participants.

Content Development

Rink (2002) has developed another framework for content development that can be useful in organizing content into progressions. She has conceptualized task progressions to include the following set of learning experiences:

1.   Informing tasks are the initial tasks in a lesson and simply describe what the students are to do. This is the beginning task in a sequence; it enables the student to explore without too much direction from the teacher.

2.   Extension tasks require the student to produce a variety of responses or to add complexity or difficulty to the selected task. For instance, the teacher could have the student throw or kick a moving ball rather than a stationary one, or throw or kick at smaller targets and increase the distance from the targets. The task-analytic procedure described in figure 2.2 is an excellent way to create a variety of exciting extension tasks.

3.   Refining tasks require the student to qualitatively improve the way she is performing a task. A refining task employs critical elements, mechanical principles, and instructional cues to focus the student's attention on refining the quality or form of the task that is being performed. For example, the student may be asked to bend and then extend the knees on the free throw in basketball or to step before swinging the bat in baseball, rather than to step while swinging.

4.   Application/assessment tasks require the student to use motor skill in an applied, competitive, or assessment setting. For example, having students participate in a modified lead-up game such as two-on-two soccer with no goalies or testing their golf skills in a pitch-and-putt task are types of application tasks.

Individualize Instruction

Once the teacher has arranged tasks from simple to complex, he or she must provide students with practice opportunities that contribute directly to successful performance and learning. Ideally, this means that all students are working at an appropriate level of difficulty and are permitted to progress at their own pace. Several models of teaching can be used to individualize instruction.

Task Instruction

Task instruction (Mosston & Ashworth, 1994; Rink, 2002) is designed to allow the student to progress through a series of tasks organized progressively from simple to complex. The tasks are typically presented on a task sheet or card. The task-analysis technique described previously is used to break the task into a series of related tasks that can be arranged from simple to complex. Students can fill out the sheet or card with partners, in small groups, or at stations.

In the task method, students progress through tasks at their own pace. Students will typically progress at different rates according to their individual abilities. Therefore, the task method is more individualized than group instruction, where all students are performing the same task at the same time. An example of a task sheet is presented in figure 2.3. In this example, math is integrated into the task sheet. In this task sheet, students work with partners so that objectives of social responsibility can also be reinforced.

In the task method, students typically select the location in the gym or on the playing field where they will perform the tasks. The task method can also be used in a station format. The gym or playing field is divided into stations, and each station has its own series of tasks arranged from simple to complex. Students can carry task sheets with them from station to station, or task cards can be displayed at the station. The students rotate to the stations during the lesson, read the task sheets or cards, and perform the activities. Task instruction is ideal for working on social responsibility goals. Students can be organized into groups, and the job of the group is to work together and cooperate to accomplish the designated tasks.

Although students are expected to read the task cards to determine what they are supposed to do, the teacher still needs to provide clear information to students about how to do the tasks. The teacher needs to make sure that the students understand the goals of the lesson by stating the objective, demonstrating skills, and providing instructional cues. (More about this is presented in chapter 4.) The teacher also needs to monitor performance of tasks and determine which students need assistance. When students need assistance, the teacher moves to the individual, group, or station where problems are occurring to provide instruction.

Pickleball Partner Task Sheet

Name_____ Partner's name_____

Date_____Grade_____

Instructions: Complete the following tasks. Each partner will perform each task before you and your partner move on to the next task. Be sure to work together to complete the tasks successfully. The mathematics equations must be solved in order to find out how many times to do each task. If you need any help, see the teacher. When you and your partner are finished with the task sheet, see the teacher about what to do next.

	Tasks	**Check when completed**

1. While standing still, bounce the ball up and down at a low level using the palm side of the racket in your dominant hand $(19 \times 4) - 52$ times.

   How many times will you do this task? _____   _____

   (Do this until you can bounce the ball without any misses. Then move on to the next task.)

2. While standing still, bounce the ball up and down at a low level using the backside of the racket in your dominant hand $(56 \div 14) \times 7$ times.

   How many times will you do this task? _____   _____

   (Do this until you can bounce the ball without any misses. Then move on to the next task.)

3. While standing still, bounce the ball up and down at a low level, alternating sides of the racket in your dominant hand $(12 \times 10) \div 15$ times.

   How many times will you do this task? _____   _____

   (Do this until you can bounce the ball without any misses. Then move on to the next task.)

4. While moving from one side of the court to the other and back again, bounce the ball up and down with the racket in your dominant hand while using one side of the racket. Go up and down the court $(56 \div 7) \div 2$ times.

   How many times will you do this task? _____   _____

   (Do this until you can bounce the ball without any misses. Then move on to the next task.)

5. While moving from one side of the court and back again, bounce the ball up and down with the racket in your dominant hand while alternating sides of the racket. Go up and down the court $(72 \div 2) \div 9$ times.

   How many times will you do this task? _____   _____

   (Do this until you can bounce the ball without any misses. Then move on to the next task.)   *(continued)*

Figure 2.3 Example of a task sheet.

Check when completed

6. From the end line, bounce the ball and serve it to your partner using your forehand so that your partner can catch the ball after one bounce. Do this 10 times.

   How many attempts were successful? _____

   What percentage is this? _____   _____

   (Do this until you get 70% of your serves in your partner's court. Then move on to the next task.)

7. From the end line, bounce the ball and serve it to your partner using your backhand so that your partner can catch the ball after one bounce. Do this 10 times.

   How many attempts were successful? _____

   What percentage is this? _____   _____

   (Do this until you get 70% of your serves in your partner's court. Then move on to the next task.)

8. Find some wall space. From a distance of 8 yards away (8 big steps), see how many times you can hit the ball against the wall in 30 seconds while using a forehand. Have your partner count while you perform. Do this 4 times.

   What was the average number of hits per minute
   that you achieved? _____   _____

9. Find some wall space. From a distance of 6 yards away (6 big steps), see how many times you can hit the ball against the wall in 30 seconds while using your backhand. Do this 4 times. Have your partner count while you perform.

   What was the average number of hits per minute
   that you achieved? _____   _____

When you finish, show your teacher this task sheet.

Figure 2.3 *(continued)*

Management is a challenge in task instruction. Students move throughout the teaching environment and work at different tasks at different times and sometimes with one or more partners. This requires more attention to management than group instruction requires, where students all do the same thing at the same time. The teacher needs to organize groups of students who will work well together when stations are used. The teacher also must design and demonstrate procedures for stopping station work, replacing station equipment, rotating to the next station, and beginning activity.

Designing the task sheets or cards is an important part of task-style instruction. Current standards in physical education stress the importance of ensuring that students receive high levels of moderate to vigorous physical activity (MVPA). Thus, task sheets or cards should enable students to spend most of their time practicing the task rather than trying to understand the task card. Therefore, the task cards should be developmentally appropriate. For example, for young students, pictures representing activities may need to be used. For older students, the task cards can be more complex, but it is probably a good idea to use brief phrases, large letters, and words that are understandable and easily read by all students in the class. Finally, it may also be helpful for the teacher to go over the tasks briefly so that the students know what they will be reading about during practice.

Reciprocal Instruction

In reciprocal teaching (Mosston & Ashworth, 1994; Rink, 2002), students assist each other in learning or performing tasks. The students evaluate and provide feedback to their partners as they perform instructional tasks. Students are taught the critical elements of the skill and instructional cues that can assist them in performing the skill. For example, the arm action in the approach in bowling would include step and push the ball away at the same time; extend ball arm, use pendulum swing to bring ball back to shoulder height; ball comes forward in pendulum swing; and ball is released as it passes vertical (Fronske, 2001). The student who is the observer would watch her partner bowl and then provide corrective or positive feedback based on these critical elements. The teacher needs to observe students to make sure that students are able to analyze the skill and give feedback that will assist their partners. An example of a reciprocal task sheet is provided in figure 2.4.

Individualized Instruction

Individualized instruction, like task and reciprocal instruction, enables students to work at their own pace on a series of progressively organized tasks. However, in individualized instruction, students engage in self-evaluation and tasks are differentiated according to difficulty so that students can select appropriate levels of performance and monitor their own progress as they move through the sequence of tasks. Evaluation of tasks can be quantitative (e.g., number of times, how long, how far) or qualitative (e.g., how well a task is done). Since students work at their own pace and decide when to progress from task to task based on self-evaluation, students frequently practice different skills or different levels of the same skill.

An individualized approach is an ideal way for implementing a fitness or conditioning component of a physical education program. For example, after a brief warm-up students can be assigned to the following stations:

1. Abdominal crunches
2. Stair steppers

Reciprocal Task Sheet

Archery

Shooter_____ Observer_____

The purpose of this task sheet is to enable you to provide your partner with feedback about appropriate form in archery. The teacher will demonstrate and review the things to look for before you begin. But you will provide the feedback, so be sure that you understand what the appropriate form looks like and how you will observe and give feedback. The checklist of things to look for goes in sequence just as the skill is performed and it is advised that you observe and record data in this sequence. If you have any problems, the teacher is always available.

The instructional task is as follows:

1. You will shoot four arrows, and your partner will give you feedback based on the "Things to look for" section below.

2. After you are finished shooting, your partner will shoot and you will observe and give feedback to your partner.

   Shooting will take place in response to the teacher's instructions. No shooting or retrieving of arrows will take place until the teacher instructs you to do so.

Things to look for when assessing archery form:

After your partner shoots four arrows, circle yes or no for each of the following form criteria. If your partner performs any of the four shots without using an element, then circle no.

Preparatory Stance and Nocking

1. Did your partner take a stance with toes along an imaginary line to the bull's-eye?   Yes   No
2. Was arrow nocked with arrow pointing down?   Yes   No
3. Was arrow nocked with the odd feather out?   Yes   No
4. Was arrow nocked below the bead?   Yes   No

Grip

5. Was grasp relaxed with the index fingertip above the arrow and the next two fingertips below the arrow?   Yes   No
6. Were thumb and little finger behind string?   Yes   No

Draw

7. Did your partner draw to a steady "T" alignment (i.e., arms up, body perpendicular to target with only head turned toward target)?   Yes   No
8. Was draw elbow extended straight back as if it were an extension of the arrow?   Yes   No

(continued)

Figure 2.4   Example of a reciprocal task sheet.

9. Was back of draw hand flat?   Yes   No

Anchor and Aim

10. Was thumb anchored on the back of the jaw in the same place each time (i.e., string dissects nose and is "kissed")?   Yes   No

11. Was left eye closed and right eye used to align arrow with bull's-eye (opposite for left-handers)?   Yes   No

12. Was anchor and aim position held for 3 seconds with breath held?   Yes   No

Release

13. Was release performed without creeping and with a gentle flick of the fingers?   Yes   No

14. Was there a follow-through where hand moves back across cheek and aiming position is held until arrow hits target?   Yes   No

Comments: What elements of your partner's performance were demonstrated in his or her performance (where you answered yes) and which ones were absent (where you answered no)? _____

_____

_____

_____

_____

_____

Figure 2.4   *(continued)*

3. Push-ups
4. Upper-body stretches
5. Triceps extensions
6. Squat thrusts
7. 10-yard (or meter) shuttle run
8. Lower-body stretches

An individualized task sheet can be designed for each student, and students can evaluate their performance during each class period and monitor their improvement across time for each exercise. An example of an individualized task sheet for conditioning is provided in figure 2.5.

Sometimes progression through an individualized instruction task sheet requires reaching a certain level of performance. For example, for an individualized task sheet on volleyball setting, the student may need to be able to successfully set a ball against a wall 8 out of 10 times before moving on to the next task, which could be setting 10 times back and forth with a partner. Individualized task sheets may also provide remedial activities if students have difficulty with certain tasks. After successful completion, the student then returns to the original hierarchy of tasks. An example of this type of individualized task sheet is provided in figure 2.6.

Learning Activity 2.2

For each of the skills analyzed in learning activity 2.1 (fielding ground balls and throwing, doing an underhand serve in volleyball, jumping rope, and throwing passes in football), use your task analysis to create either a task sheet, reciprocal task sheet, or an individual program. Make sure you try each method of instruction at least once.

Individualized Conditioning Task Sheet

Individualized Station Lesson

Name _____ Date_____

Indicate your level of performance for each of the following tasks. **Stretching stations are rest stations and are not evaluated.**

	DAYS														
	1	2	3	4	5	6	7	8	9	10	11	12	13	14	15
Station 1. **Crunches.** How many in 60 seconds?															
Station 2. **Stair steps.** How many steps in 60 seconds?															

(continued)

Figure 2.5   Individualized conditioning task sheet.

	DAYS														
	1	2	3	4	5	6	7	8	9	10	11	12	13	14	15
Station 3. **Push-ups.** How many in 60 seconds?															
Station 4. **Upper-body stretch.** Perform a stretching exercise for deltoids and the pectoralis major.															
Station 5. **Triceps extension.** How many in 60 seconds?															
Station 6. **Squat thrusts.** How many in 60 seconds?															
Station 7. **10-yard (meter) shuttle run.** How many runs in 60 seconds?															
Station 8. **Lower-body stretch.** Perform a stretching exercise for the quadriceps and hamstrings.															

Figure 2.5 *(continued)*

Name _____ Date_____

Complete the following tasks. Be sure to concentrate on the proper form for the set. **Things to look for (critical elements):** Hands form a basket, thumbs and fingers are in the shape of a heart, hands are up and elbows are out, look through the heart, and rapidly catch and throw (*do not* slap or poke the ball with the fingers).

1. Toss ball to yourself and set the ball at least 10 feet high (3 meters, or twice your height) and catch it while staying within a hula hoop. Do this 10 times. Record the number of successes. _____ If fewer than 8, repeat task. If you had 8 or more, go to task 2.

2a. Stand 3 to 4 feet (about 1 meter to 1.2 meters) from a wall. Toss the ball up, set the ball to the wall above the 10-foot line, and catch the rebound without stepping out of a hula hoop. Do this 10 times. Record the number of successes. _____ If fewer than 8, try task 2b. If 8 or more, go to task 3.

2b. Do task 2a, but set the ball below the 10-foot line at a height that is comfortable. When you get 8 out of 10, go back to task 2a.

3a. Stand 3 to 4 feet from a wall. Toss the ball up and set the ball to the wall above the 10-foot line. Set the ball 5 consecutive times without moving more than one step. Record the number of successes. _____ If fewer than 4, try task 3b. If 4 or more, go to task 4.

3b. Do task 3a, but set the ball below the 10-foot line at a height that is comfortable. When you get 4 out of 5, go back to task 3a.

4. Stand 3 to 4 feet from a wall. Toss the ball up and set the ball to the wall above the 10-foot line. Set the ball 8 consecutive times without moving more than one step. Record the number of consecutive successes. _____ Keep trying until you get at least 6 consecutive sets.

When you successfully complete task 4, see your teacher for further instructions.

Figure 2.6 Individualized task sheet for volleyball set.

Adjust (Individualize) Tasks Based on Students' Skill Level

Although the teacher may have designed a wonderful lesson that is highly individualized, students may still need assistance in learning. Each student comes to the lesson or practice session with different prior experiences, interests, and abilities. Therefore, the teacher may need to adjust or modify tasks to enable the student to be more successful. In the following text, two techniques are described for efficiently assisting students in adjusting task difficulty, as suggested by Graham (2001). Of course, as mentioned previously, students are very good at task analysis and should be encouraged to solve their motor problems themselves whenever possible.

Intratask Variation

The teacher and students need to continually assess performance during the lesson so that appropriate challenges can be developed. During lessons, if a student is having difficulty performing, the teacher (or the student, if they have been instructed in intratask variation) can decrease the level of difficulty of the task. Conversely, if the task is too easy, the teacher can increase the difficulty of the task. The teacher can mentally use the task-analysis procedure (described previously) to modify task difficulty as the student is performing. Often the teacher can make these adjustments by directing the student to do the task higher or lower, farther or closer, faster or slower, with a longer or shorter implement, or with a larger or smaller ball or target. The teacher can also adjust the difficulty level by modifying the qualitative aspects of performance (i.e., refinement tasks). For example, the teacher can instruct the student to focus on the critical elements of the skill rather than being concerned with the outcome that is achieved. These and other adjustments that can be used for quickly increasing or decreasing the difficulty of tasks for individual students are called intratask variations.

Teaching by Invitation

Teaching by invitation is another effective way of individualizing instruction. This method allows students to modify tasks. When teaching by invitation, the teacher structures the task so that the student can manipulate the dimensions of the task. For example, instead of placing a single cone at a certain distance away from a target of only one size and requiring the student to throw a 6-inch (15 cm) playground ball at the target, the teacher would have two cones, one close to large, medium-sized, and small targets placed at various heights on the wall, and one far away from the targets. Finally, the student would be able to choose from a variety of objects, such as a 6-inch (15 cm) playground ball, tennis balls, beanbags, and Nerf balls.

The teacher's goal is to encourage the student to make choices about task dimensions that will facilitate successful performance. The student is encouraged to select the distance, target size and height, and type of object that will facilitate successful (i.e., about 70% accuracy) performance. Of course, the teacher would still assist the student who is trying tasks that are too easy or too difficult by using intratask variation. The difference is that when using teaching by invitation, teachers encourage students to think for themselves and modify their task choices based on assessment of their own performance.

Equipment should also be appropriately matched to the size, skill, and confidence level of the learner. Even if there are enough regulation basketballs for all students, they may be too large and too heavy for young students and students with less ability. Providing a variety of balls will allow students to choose the ball that best meets their needs. When teaching any activity, an instructor should have several variations in equipment (sizes, weights, or lengths) available to accommodate individual differences. Elementary students will also have more success if equipment will not hurt them. Smaller, lighter, and softer balls, such as Nerf balls, can be used effectively in decreasing the fear of injury that accompanies the use of harder, heavier, "regulation" balls and equipment.

Matching equipment size to the learners' skill level is important for successful performance.

Make Sure Students Are Ready Before Playing Games

Games are an important component of physical education. Games offer students an opportunity to apply motor skills in sport settings, learn to compete (i.e., win and lose graciously), work cooperatively with teammates, respect rules, become physically fit, and gain lifetime skills in sports that they can maintain in adulthood (Beets & Pitetti, 2005). NASPE has developed guidelines for determining appropriate and inappropriate instructional practices at the elementary (NASPE, 2000), middle school (NASPE, 2001), and high school (NASPE, 2004) levels that are related to games instruction. Following is a list of the developmentally appropriate and inappropriate characteristics of games instruction. Teachers and coaches should use these guidelines when selecting or designing game experiences.

Appropriate Practice

1. Games are selected, designed, sequenced, and modified by teachers or children to maximize the learning and enjoyment of the children.

2. Teachers or children modify official rules and regulations of adult sports to match the varying abilities of the children.

3. *All* children are involved in activities that allow them to continuously remain active.

4. Teams are formed in ways that preserve the dignity and self-respect of every child. For example, a teacher privately forms teams by using knowledge of children's skill abilities, or the children form teams cooperatively or randomly.

5. Children participate in team games (two or three per team) that allow for numerous practice opportunities while also allowing them to learn about the various aspects of the game being taught.

6. Activities emphasize self-improvement, participation, and cooperation instead of winning and losing.

7. Teachers are aware of the nature of competition and do not require higher levels of game play from children before they are ready. For example, children are allowed to choose between a game in which score is kept and one that is just for fun.

Inappropriate Practice

1. Games are taught with no obvious purpose or goal other than to keep children busy, happy, and good or to have fun for the duration of the lesson.

2. Official, adult rules of team sports govern the activities in physical education classes, resulting in low rates of success and enjoyment for many children.

3. Children are eliminated with no chance to reenter the activity, or they must sit for long periods. For example, games such as duck, duck, goose; dodgeball; and elimination tag provide limited opportunities for many children, especially the slower, less agile ones.

4. Teams are formed by "captains" selecting one child at a time, thereby exposing the lower-skilled children to peer ridicule.

5. Teams are formed by pitting boys against the girls, thereby emphasizing gender differences rather than cooperation.

6. Children participate in full-sided games (e.g., the class of 30 is split into two teams of 15 and these two teams play each other), thereby leading to few practice opportunities.

7. Children are *required* to participate in activities that label children as winners and losers.

8. Children are *required* to participate in activities that compare one child's performance against others (e.g., a race in which the winning child is clearly identified).

Reprinted from *Appropriate Practices for Elementary School Physical Education* (2000), *Appropriate Practices for Middle School Physical Education* (2001), and *Appropriate Practices for High School Physical Education* (2004), with permission from the National Association for Sport and Physical Education (NASPE), 1900 Association Drive, Reston, VA 20191, USA.

Modify Games to Be Developmentally Appropriate

As stated above, it may be inappropriate for students to engage in full-sided games in which adult rules and regulations are applied. If students have not gained proficiency at performing individual skills and skills in basic combinations, it is unlikely that students will be able to participate in the actual game with a reasonable level of success and enjoyment. Described below are strategies for modifying and teaching games progressively so that student success and fun are maximized.

Structure of Games

Teachers need to be able to analyze game structures and select and modify games to facilitate the achievement of educational goals. Games are composed of a variety of elements (Hawkins, 2000; Morris & Stiehl, 1999).

For example, games vary in terms of their purpose. The purpose of net games (e.g., tennis, badminton, volleyball) is to deflect objects over a net into the opponent's area in ways that prevent the opponent from returning the objects. The purpose of invasion games (e.g., soccer) is to enter another team's territory and score a goal by projecting, deflecting, or carrying an object into a goal area or across a goal line. Target games (e.g., darts), fielding games (e.g., softball), chasing games (e.g., tag), or racing games (e.g., 100-yard dash) also have different purposes.

Although games are designed for a specific purpose, it is acceptable to alter the purpose of a game to accomplish developmentally appropriate goals. For example, in invasion games such as soccer, points might be awarded for kicking a ball over the end line rather than inside a goal. Also, in net games such as tennis, the purpose could be changed to give points for each successful serve and forehand regardless of who ultimately wins the point.

Games vary according to the rules and skills that are employed. Game modifications based on changing rules might involve reducing the number of rules to make the game simpler or changing rules to promote greater participation. For example, in volleyball, a teacher might permit beginners at the elementary level to catch the ball in order to increase success, as in the game newcomb. To make games more accessible to beginners, distances between bases in softball can be shortened, the length of the field in football can be decreased, the size of the goal in lacrosse may be made larger, or a soccer game can even be played without goalies to increase scoring.

Equipment can also be modified to simplify games. In volleyball, balloons, beach balls, or Nerf balls might be used. Large bats can be used in tee ball. Smaller basketballs that fit the hands of students can be used instead of regulation-sized balls.

Finally, teachers can vary the number and organization of players. Teachers can decrease numbers of the official game, thereby increasing student involvement. Playing several 5-on-5 or even 3-on-3 games, rather than a single, full-sided game of soccer in which there are 11 students on a team, will increase levels of participation. Teachers need to consider and analyze the key elements of a game's structure to determine whether the game is developmentally appropriate or if the game should be modified to better achieve educational goals. These game elements can even be taught to students so they can design or modify games themselves.

Learning Activity 2.3

Go to the library and find descriptions of five games. Analyze the games and decide whether they are developmentally appropriate or if they need to be rejected or modified. If the games need to be modified, describe how to do the modification.

Progressions in Teaching Games

Rink (2002) provides a strategy for games instruction that consists of four progressive stages of instruction.

• **Stage 1: Object control.** Individual skills form the foundation for game play. In stage 1, students would receive instruction and practice in the individual skills required in a game. In basketball, for example, one task would be dribbling; other tasks would be passing (bounce, chest), shooting on goal (set, jump, layups), and free throws. In this stage, the teacher needs to assist the students in becoming proficient in individual skills such as projections, deflections, receptions, and carrying or maintaining control of objects as indicated in chapter 1 (see table 1.2). Task analyses would be used to increase the difficulty of the task and move the student progressively toward the efficient control of the object (for example at various speeds, distances, while stationary and moving, and with partners).

• **Stage 2: Complexity added.** In this stage students combine the skills that would be used in game play and begin working cooperatively with teammates. Students receive instruction and practice in using several skills as they are used in game-like situations, with an emphasis on making smooth transitions between the skill combinations. For example, a basketball task combining many individual skills might be a 2-on-1 (give-and-go) activity where the student dribbles past an opponent and passes to a teammate. When the opponent follows the ball to the teammate, the student will break toward the hoop, receive a pass back from the teammate, and execute a layup or a jump shot. The goal of adding complexity is for students to become proficient in combining and controlling skills before moving to game play involving strategies.

• **Stage 3: Strategies and rules.** After individual skills and combinations of skills have been learned and internalized to a point where students can allocate attention to other aspects of the game than only the skills, they are taught the rules and the offensive and defensive strategies of playing the game. If a student can dribble a basketball only by fully attending to the skill, he will not be able to observe the game environment and attend to the strategic elements of the game, such as where his teammates and opponents are on the court, which teammate is open for a pass, or when they might be open for a shot when dribbling. In stage 3 basic offensive and defensive strategies are taught in a progressive manner, going from simple to more complex.

A task structure suggested by Hawkins (2000) that could be used for games in which students need to pass a ball to open players has three students at four corners of a square, with one corner open. A student passes the ball to one of the other students and runs to the open corner. The student who receives the ball passes to another student and runs to the newly vacated corner, and so on. This teaches the strategy of moving to open space and getting open when a player does not have the ball. A subsequent task could be to place a defender in the middle of the square. Then, the student passing the ball would have to select the player who is open and pass to that player. This task structure could be used for hockey, soccer, basketball, or any sport where passing and moving to open spaces is a key strategy. Stage 3 enables students to become proficient in the rules and strategies of game play before immersion in the actual game.

• **Stage 4: Game play.** In this stage students play the regulation game or a modified lead-up or simulation of the actual game. Students use most of the rules and are reasonably proficient at performing the skills and skill combinations. Students have internalized the basic offensive and defensive strategies, and the game looks like the "real thing." Students may assume responsibility for different positions (e.g., soccer goalie, attacker, and defender). The teacher would continue to teach during game play by modifying the game as described in the previous section if student performance levels decrease, stopping play for instruction (i.e., chalk talks) or allowing play to continue until a stopping point and then providing students with feedback (Metzler, 1990). The important point is that teaching does not end once the games begin.

Teaching Games for Understanding

In contrast to the progressive skill-development approach described above, advocates of the Teaching Games for Understanding (TGfU) (Griffin, Mitchell, & Oslin, 1997) model emphasize student understanding of the purpose or aim of classes of game types (i.e., target, net, invasion, fielding), the general strategies associated with a class of games (i.e., changing pace, spreading the field, exploiting opponent's weaknesses, and the like), and tactics (i.e., moving to open spaces, leading the receiver, and the like) that often are applicable across games within a class, but may apply to many games regardless of class (e.g., feinting or faking is common to all games), prior to learning the skills needed to implement the strategies and tactics.

There are three reasons TGfU adopts the tactics-before-skills approach. First, traditional games instruction has often been characterized by lengthy skill instruction in which students are expected to practice without an opportunity to apply skills in game-like settings. Research (Holt, Strean, & Bengoechea, 2002) as well as intuition supports the notion that students of all ages like and want to be involved in games. Therefore, it makes good instructional sense to motivate students by involving them in game-like experiences.

Second, by placing students in tactical situations they are able to appreciate the aim or purpose of the game and develop a tactical awareness early in the instructional process. Skills are more salient when understood from a tactical perspective, rather than practicing skills without an understanding of why the skill is being learned. Students are confronted with modified game-like tasks that exemplify the various tactics of the game, and in this way they are ready to address the technical skills involved in the sport with an appreciation for how they are used for tactical purposes.

Third, the TGfU approach assumes that strategies and tactics will transfer to other games within a type. The idea is that a student who has an understanding of the strategic and tactical elements of basketball will also have an implicit understanding of other invasion games such as soccer, field hockey, and ultimate. There are skills that also are transferable from both tactical and critical element perspectives. For example, a cross-over dribble in basketball is used to pass a defender by moving the ball from one hand to the other so the dribbler's body protects the ball from the defender. The step-over dribble, used by Renaldo to set the scoring record in the 2006 World Cup against Ghana, has the same tactical purpose: redirecting the ball in order to move the ball past a defender. In many invasion games there are similar strategies for moving an object past a defender by rapidly changing direction. In addition, concepts like moving to open space, feinting, spreading the field and skill patterns like projections (e.g., passes, shots), deflections (e.g., kicking, striking), and receptions (e.g., catching, trapping) share common elements and apply broadly to a variety of invasion games. Thus, TGfU makes the transitions to new games more cognitively efficient and meaningful as students are able to use prior strategic, tactical, and skill knowledge to inform the process of learning new applications of that knowledge.

So, what does the TGfU approach to teaching look like? Let's take a look at invasion games. The aim of all invasion games is to move an object through an opponent's territory by passing, dribbling, and carrying the object, and then to score points by throwing, kicking, striking, or carrying the object across a goal line or into a netted goal, while prohibiting the opponent from doing the same.

Tactics for invasion games would include "moving to open spaces" so that opportunities to pass an object downfield or to take open shots on goal are created. Faking or feinting is also a general tactic that can be seen in the pump-fake in football, the head-fake in basketball, and the cut-back or fake shot dribble in soccer. Other general tactics for invasion games are presented in table 2.2 (Griffin, Mitchell, & Oslin, 1997).

An example of a tactical lead-up game for invasion games that might be used is "three passes." The goal is for a team to obtain a point by simply passing an object among three different teammates. Of course, this is made more difficult by defenders who are attempting to intercept or knock down the object. All players can move except the player with the object. This game emphasizes the offensive tactics of "moving to open spaces and spreading the field" to create openings for passes ("leading the receiver when throwing the ball"), and the defensive tactics of "marking or guarding a player"

Table 2.2   Examples of Tasks for Teaching Tactics

Game type	Offensive tactics	Defensive tactics
Invasion games	Controlling ball or object · Shield ball or object.	Stealing ball or object · Keep hands up and ready.
	Moving ball or object into opponent's side of field · Pass to teammates. · Move to open spaces. · Spread out in the field. · Use triangle formations. · Cross over.	Prohibiting the movement of a ball or object into your space · Mark players. · Cut off opponents. · Double-team. · Use zones or 1 on 1. · Spin or reach around.
	Attacking the opponent's goal · Give and go. · Use angles of attack.	Defending your goal · Switch positions. · Cut down angles.

From J.L. Griffin, S.A. Mitchell, and J.L. Oslin, 1997, *Teaching sport concepts and skills: A tactical games approach* (Champaign, IL: Human Kinetics).

and "switching attention" back and forth between the thrower and the person being guarded.

This can be used as a lead-up, tactical game for basketball at the upper elementary and secondary levels, depending on the ability levels of the students. Various objects could be used, culminating in the use of basketballs. Since the goal in basketball is to move the ball down the court into the opposition's territory and score goals, the game could be adjusted to add various types and numbers of goals that are developmentally appropriate, so that the game now requires the students to move the object toward a goal to score. Ultimately, you may add dribbling to passing as another means of moving the ball down court and use actual basketballs and goals, if developmentally appropriate.

The challenge when teaching for tactical understanding is to arrange tasks so that they illuminate certain tactical ideas. It is suggested that game tasks exaggerate the tactical concept by modifying tasks. Following are other examples of these types of tasks.

- **Toss tennis, badminton, and volleyball.** Doolittle (1995) suggests having students toss and catch balls from opposite sides of the court when teaching beginning students. In this game students can get the idea of placing the object away from the opponent before they begin to learn difficult striking skills. The court can also be adjusted so that students learn the importance of the front-to-back and side-to-side strategies of playing net games. For example, a court can be set up so that students use only the front half, so their best tactical option is moving the opponent from side to side. Or the court can be set up so that it is long and narrow, emphasizing the importance of moving the opponent up and back. Eventually, when students understand the tactical elements of the game, striking skills can be introduced. However, even at this point it is possible that equipment modifications can be made to ease the transition to the actual game. For example, pickleball can serve as a lead-up to tennis. Students have immediate success using the short pickleball racket and a Wiffle ball, even on a tennis court. It is possible to revisit the front-to-back and side-to-side tasks with the new equipment; then, after sufficient success, the students can progress to using actual tennis rackets and tennis balls.

• **Go-to-the-goal games.** Williams and Ayers (2000) provide suggestions for arranging 2-on-1 tasks that enable the students to experience a variety of tactics used in invasion games. For example, a 2-on-1 task that requires students to move toward a ball down the field toward a target can be used to emphasize the following offensive and defensive tactics:

Offensive Tactics: Player With the Ball

1. Pass quickly when a teammate is open.
2. Change direction and speeds, and use feints to shake defender.
3. Lead teammate to keep ball moving forward.

Offensive Tactics: Player Without the Ball

1. Move into open space to receive the pass.
2. Move toward the target.
3. Move to meet the ball.

Defensive Tactics

1. Stay between the target and offensive players.
2. Move to force the pass.
3. Force opponent away from the target.
4. Use feints to invite premature passes and intercept.

As a follow-up activity, a 2-on-1 task against a goalie would add tactics related to defending the goals by cutting down angles and reducing goal size by moving to the offensive players. Offensive tactics include waiting for the goalie to commit and then passing, using feints and fake shots to achieve open shots, and using a give-and-go strategy to get an open shot on goal.

So, which is the best way to teach: the skill-development model or the TGfU approach? The answer is both. Our view is that tactics need to be understood to make skill meaningful and skill must be learned to make the application of tactics successful. It is the skill-tactic link that is critical.

The important point is that students need to understand early in instruction what the purpose of the skill is and how it can be applied to improve competence in game play. Students need to know why they are doing what they are doing.

Skills and tactics should be taught in a blended way so that there is a seamless connection between skills-tactic linkages and each lesson or practice session contributes to the student's increasing understanding of this relationship. The teacher also needs to appreciate that the student is engaged in the process of constructing or reconstructing knowledge structures or game representations by learning the "language" of the sport. That is, students are busy constructing the declarative (rules, positions, field/court properties, names of skills, and so on), procedural (tactics, if–then conditions for skills-tactic links, and the like), and strategic knowledge (aim, purpose, and approaches of game types) that will enable them to "read" (i.e., process) the wealth of information available in the game environment. Of course, this can be a difficult process for students and the teacher may need to cue, demonstrate, and explain how strategies, tactics, and skills transfer from one game to another as they engage students in tasks that illuminate the transferability of game elements. Ultimately, as gamespersonship evolves, students would be able to use their knowledge structures to efficiently direct their own learning and performance by monitoring their information processing (e.g., attention, planning, execution, evaluation, and storage of information) via the direct, conscious control of their own cognitive processes.

Whether the teacher begins a lesson or practice with a skill or tactical focus would depend on the needs of the students. If the students have learned the rudiments of the skill and can be successful in a tactical activity, then the teacher could get the students started immediately in the tactical activity. However, if the students are less skilled, it may be appropriate to begin a lesson with skill instruction and then move to the tactical activity with continued attention to skill refinement. The teacher could also modify the skill used to increase success (e.g., substituting a beach ball for a volleyball), and then teach using the actual object after the tactical activity. There is also no reason why skills couldn't be reviewed during the introductory warm-up segment of the lesson, so the teacher could check to see the skill levels of the students before introducing the tactical game. For example, for the "three passes" game described above, a "toss tag" game could be played where students must continuously toss an object in a stationary (frozen) position when tagged. Or a partner throwing-and-catching station could be a rest station in a series of fitness stations, in a warm-up. In either case the teacher can check to see that students can throw or catch prior to teaching the skill and the associated tactical task.

The point is that there is a flow back and forth between tactical and skill foci throughout a lesson and unit as the teacher responds to students' needs and moves them toward skillful and tactical game play. The skill-development approach provides effective cues and practice activities for skill learning and the tactical approach offers wonderful tasks that illuminate the tactical and strategic dimensions of game play and make skill learning meaningful and fun. The key is to do both without spending an inordinate amount of time on either.

Learning Activity 2.4

Interview a coach of an invasion, net or wall, target, or fielding sport and find out what tasks the coach uses for teaching tactics in the sport.

Sport Education

Sport education (SE) is an exciting curricular model. The assumption underlying SE is that sport is an integral part of our culture and the intent is to provide students with authentic sporting experiences that enable them to become "literate" sportspersons (Siedentop, 1994). Students become literate by assuming a variety of roles in SE classes, which are structured very differently from traditional physical education units and provide alternative assessment strategies that reward students not only for learning skills and contributing to successful team performance but also for successfully completing the multiple roles that are built into the class design. The research that has been conducted on the SE model indicates that students like the model better than traditional physical education and that it is effective in facilitating engagement and learning in both coed and single-gender classes (Hastie, 1998; 2000). The following are the seven features that characterize SE:

1. **Seasons.** Traditional physical education is typically organized around short (3- to 5-week) units. This does not provide the in-depth learning experience that students need in order to become truly competent and literate sportspersons. SE is organized around seasons that are longer than traditional units and afford students the opportunity to become immersed in the sporting experience.

2. **Affiliation.** A key element of SE is the team membership and the social skills that occur during the season. Practicing skills, learning about the tactics of the sport, and engaging in scrimmages and formal competition are all opportunities for students to work together. In traditional physical education, team membership constantly changes and students are often selected each day with the use of procedures that are embarrassing and stigmatizing, such as having students select teammates. In SE, however, students are assigned to teams via a selection

process that is humane and supportive, and team membership lasts for the entire season. Thus, students gain a long-term affiliation with their teams and team members.

3. **Formal competition.** During the season, teams are engaged in a formal schedule of practices, scrimmages, and competition. This structure emphasizes the importance of practice sessions and encourages students to improve their skills and learn strategies in preparation for formal competition.

4. **Culminating event.** In SE a culminating event (or season finale) that involves all participants is essential. This event provides students with a tangible incentive for working hard at learning the sport all season long.

5. **Multiple roles.** The intent of SE is to provide students with authentic sporting experiences that enable them to become literate sportspersons. Students become literate by assuming a variety of roles in SE, such as official, team publicist, statistician, photographer, Web designer, and strength and fitness trainer, in addition to the role of team member and participant. Participants assume a variety of roles throughout the practice season and during formal competition. To hold students accountable, points are often awarded for their performance of roles, and these points contribute to the final achievement of the team. Thus, a student who is very good at statistics or Web research might garner as many points for the team as the top scorer.

6. **Record keeping.** Keeping and publicly displaying records emphasize the importance of working as a team to achieve success. SE provides recognition to students and teams for success. Records are kept and publicized for the various roles that students assume and the artifacts that they produce during the season. So, success is defined not only as performance during the end-of-season event but also for the products (statistical records, team history, photographs, Web sites, and the like) that are crafted during the season and the roles that students assumed.

7. **Festivity.** In SE, a festive atmosphere should pervade the entire season. The environment in SE should include videotaping, awards ceremonies, team names and colors, and posters that emphasize the celebration of teamwork, humane competition, good sporting behavior, and improvement.

Learning Activity 2.5

Create a plan for applying the sport education model to a specific sport. Incorporate each of the features of sport education in your plan.

Summary

In this chapter a variety of strategies are presented to assist teachers in designing and modifying tasks to increase students' success. Techniques such as creating task progressions, selecting and modifying games, using individualized instruction, adjusting tasks using intratask variation, and teaching by invitation are presented.

Design Tasks That Are Fun, Engaging, and Safe

In order for tasks to be engaging, they need to be interesting and *fun*. Research (Hidi, 1990; 2000) indicates that interest in content is a critical variable in determining how people select, attend to, and process certain types of information. Students who are provided with learning experiences that are interesting to them approach subject matter with greater attention and depth of processing. Fortunately, research indicates that students enjoy physical education. Goodlad (1984), in his classic study of American education, found that 86.9% of elementary, 80.1% of junior high, and 79.8% of senior high students stated that they liked physical education. Unfortunately, students like physical education less as they get older. Anyone who has spent any time in middle school and high school gyms can attest to the fact that students can become disinterested in physical education unless a concerted effort is made to design tasks that are interesting and fun.

In the area of physical education, researchers have found that students vary in their perceptions of how interesting various tasks are (McKenzie, Alcaraz, & Sallis, 1994). Research (Chen, 2001; Chen, Darst, & Pangrazi, 2001; Chen & Ennis, 2004) indicates that there appear to be five major dimensions of situational interest that can influence the appeal of learning tasks to students: novelty (i.e., new or fresh tasks), challenge (i.e., complex or demanding tasks), attention demand (i.e., tasks that grab or demand attention), instant enjoyment (i.e., appealing or exciting tasks), and exploration intention (i.e., tasks that stimulate analysis, inquiry, or discovery). Situational interest is believed to affect personal interest by engendering a long-lasting interest in a subject area, particularly if learning tasks are high in situational interest and an ongoing part of the curriculum. As Chen and Ennis (2004) argue, "As a function of learning-task design, situational interest plays a critical role in motivating students to engage actively in learning" (p. 336). A number of strategies can be used to make instructional tasks enjoyable for students. In fact, most of the task design strategies mentioned throughout this text will make tasks more interesting and fun for students. Upon completion of this chapter, the teacher should be able to do the following:

1. Incorporate variety into instructional tasks.
2. Incorporate goals or challenges into instructional tasks.
3. Incorporate inherent feedback into instructional tasks.
4. Incorporate student choice into instructional tasks.
5. Structure integrated instructional tasks.
6. Incorporate music into instructional tasks.
7. Design tasks that reduce physical and emotional danger.

Design Tasks That Provide Variety

Variety is the spice of life. This is especially true in physical education. Providing students with an array of tasks can make physical education more challenging and interesting for students. Practicing skills in a variety of contexts can assist students in building large, flexible knowledge structures that enable students to apply the skills in a variety of situations. Recent research on the effects of contextual interference indicates that students attend more diligently and retain information longer when practice takes place in settings where students are required to practice skills in a variety of situations rather than practicing a single skill in the same way throughout a lesson. It is thought that when a new skill or a different practice context is introduced, the student must refocus attention to the new task, and this increases retention. Conversely, when tasks are redundant, the student loses attention, and the positive effects of practice diminish (Magill, 2004; Magill & Hall, 1990).

The task analysis approach described in chapter 2 can be used to increase variety in lessons or practice sessions. Providing a variety of challenging activities will reduce the possibility of boring students with the same types of tasks presented over and over again. If tasks are not interesting for the learners, they will find other things to do and that can often be in the form of off-task behavior. Tasks are composed of many variables, and altering these variables by using task analysis enables the teacher to literally generate hundreds of tasks that bring variety to lessons and practice sessions. Students are also very good at analyzing tasks, and including the students in the task-analytic process can add to their interest in the subject matter of sport and physical education.

Learning Activity 3.1

In small groups, conduct a task analysis for serving a volleyball. Ask yourself, "What elements can make serving a volleyball easier or more difficult to perform?" See how many different ways of serving a volleyball you can identify. If you do not exceed several hundred, you are not thinking hard enough about all of the ways one can serve a volleyball.

Teachers can increase variety by providing various teaching methods. In addition to the methods described in chapter 2, using a range of teaching methods, including cooperative learning, problem solving, and guided discovery, can bring variety to lessons and emphasize the cognitive dimension of learning. More about these methods will be provided in chapter 4.

Challenging students to solve problems can stimulate students' interest and increase their engagement in learning skills. For example, students may be asked to explore the variety of ways to move a soccer ball down the field. Students would experiment and solve this problem with a variety of ideas (e.g., dribbling, passing, heading, and the like) that would expand their understanding of the possible ways to "move a soccer ball down the field." Also, having students create instructional video clips for class, search the Internet and share pertinent Web sites, engage in peer or cross-age

Encouraging students to search the Internet and share their findings with their peers is a way of integrating variety in teaching methods.

tutoring—even permitting students to choose instructional tasks, strategies, or equipment—are viable alternative methods that the teacher could use to integrate variety into her approach to teaching.

Design Tasks That Have Goals or Challenges

Tasks that have goals or challenges are more engaging for students. Often teachers simply ask students to practice a skill on their own or with a partner and expect the students to stay on task. Though students may persist even when asked to simply do a task, teachers can make task engagement more likely by providing goals or challenges that will stimulate learners to persist with a task. Using task challenges such as number of attempts, time, speed, accuracy, and distance can provide students with specific goals to try to achieve. For example, time can be used by challenging the student to "see if you can jog for 4 minutes without slowing to a walk." Also, accuracy can be used by asking students to "see how many free throws out of 10 can you score," distance can be used to challenge students to "see how far can you throw a softball," and speed can be used to ask students to "see how fast can you dribble a soccer ball the width of the field and back again."

Design Tasks That Provide Inherent Feedback

Inherent feedback is an integral part of the task and results when the student successfully performs the task (Herkowitz, 1978). For example, the sound that the pins make in bowling when hit by the ball is inherent feedback and provides the student with feedback that the task has been performed successfully. Noises associated with many tasks in sport and physical education provide information regarding success, and noise is also motivational and engaging. In addition to noise, movement of equipment can be an effective form of inherent feedback. For example, targets that can be knocked down when struck successfully can be engaging for students. Color can be used when designing tasks. Making certain heights or distances various colors can give students concrete goals to try to achieve, and thus make tasks more engaging. A task that incorporates inherent feedback as part of the task structure will generally increase interest and participation among students.

Design Tasks That Permit Choice

Ideally, students will be provided with a variety of activities in their physical education programs: fitness education activities such as aerobics, power walking, cycling, yoga, and aquatic exercise; outdoor activities such as hiking, backpacking, mountain biking, and orienteering; recreational activities such as in-line skating or ice skating, archery, and golf; martial arts such as karate, taekwondo, and tai chi; and traditional activities such as football, soccer, basketball, and soccer.

The point is that students have different abilities and interests, and if teachers can provide students with an opportunity to choose activities that match their abilities and interests, they will certainly feel a greater level of enjoyment. In fact, in a recent study by Condon and Collier (2002), a survey of students' preferred activities was used to allow students' input regarding programmatic content. Students then were able to choose the activities that were of greatest interest to them. The researchers found that students appreciated having a choice and concluded that students pay more attention, put forth more effort, and find physical education more enjoyable when they have a choice.

Even in situations where students' choice of curricular option may be limited because of lack of facilities, requirements for teaching certain curricula, or unwilling colleagues, teachers can provide students with choice. Teaching by invitation, discussed in chapter 2, is an effective way of permitting students to make choices. In this method, the teacher's task is to encourage students to make choices among the dimensions of the equipment and settings that will facilitate successful (70% to 80% success rates) task performance. Teachers encourage students to think for themselves and modify their task choices based on their analysis of their own performance.

Structure Integrated Tasks

Integration in physical education can be fun. Physical education, perhaps more than any other content area, has the potential to enliven and bring relevance to academic content. There are several reasons that physical education is well suited for teaching academic content. Recall and comprehension of interesting content are superior to that of less interesting material. Since students like physical education, physical education would be an ideal vehicle for teaching with academic content.

A second reason for using physical education as a vehicle for teaching academic content is that physical education is currently one of the few active content areas in school curricula. Students learn actively by doing rather than by simply listening. Goodlad (1984) points out that in academic settings, "there is a paucity of demonstrating, showing, and modeling on the part of teachers and constructing things, acting things out, carrying out projects, and the like on the part of the students" (p. 115). In contrast, Goodlad found that physical education is characterized by less passive seatwork and more active learning than in academic subjects.

Third, it is a false dichotomy to consider language arts, mathematics, science, and history as academic subjects and physical education as nonacademic. As Lawson (1987) has pointed out, physical education is composed of a rich, sophisticated body of knowledge that includes virtually all of the content offered elsewhere in school curricula as academic. For example, certified physical education teachers have completed courses such as exercise physiology, anatomy and kinesiology, sport history, sociology and psychology, measurement and evaluation, nutrition, and first aid. Certified physical education teachers are also equipped to use the gymnasium and playing fields as laboratories for teaching this knowledge. In fact, teaching knowledge from the academic disciplines along with the traditional fitness- and skill-oriented mission of physical education has been advocated for a number of years (Housner, 2001; Kneer, 1981; Nelson & Cline, 1987; Placek, 2003; Werner & Burton, 1979).

Finally, integrating other subject matter into physical education is fun for students. Following are examples of learning tasks that can be incorporated into the physical education program either in isolation or as an integrated component of the overall educational curriculum. It is important to note that integration should not reduce the time allocated to psychomotor, affective, and fitness objectives. Rather, academic concepts logically related to the cognitive objectives of the physical education program should be the focus of integration. These concepts can also be taught primarily by classroom teachers and reinforced in physical education as a collaborative effort to integrate the curriculum.

Science

The emphasis in physical education on the structure and function of the human body, particularly in response to exercise, suggests that integration with courses in biology would be effective. Students actually experience anatomy and physiology as they are tested for cardiovascular (heart and blood vessels) and cardiorespiratory (heart and lungs) adaptation to exercise. Scientifically based prescriptions to remediate deficiencies in cardiac function would inform students of the findings of medical research regarding the principles of frequency, intensity, and time that underlie the attainment of a training effect (i.e., increased stroke volume, decreased blood pressure, and reduced resting and exercise heart rates). Assessments and prescriptions in the areas of muscular strength, percent body fat, and flexibility would also inform the students of the anatomical and physiological underpinnings of these health-related dimensions of human biological performance.

Biomechanics is the study of the principles of physics as they apply to human movement. Athletic skills can be characterized as the completion of a specific movement outcome through the adaptation of the musculoskeletal system to the physical laws of nature inherent in our physical environment. The human body is a system of levers that attempts to overcome the physical constraints of gravity, inertia, and friction and to impart sufficient linear or angular force either on itself or on external objects to accomplish a designated outcome. Many of the kinesiological principles discussed in chapter 1 can be used in integrating the curriculum and providing high-quality physical education at the same time. Teaching scientific laws, such as Newton's laws of motion, through scientific investigation of sport-skill performance offers many advantages. Perhaps the most important is providing the student with a vehicle for understanding physics principles. Using students' movements to generate the data for scientific biomechanical analysis provides them with a sense of ownership and relevance in the scientific enterprise. What data could be more personal than one's own movement? These data should be among the most relevant that the physics or physical education teacher could use for scientific experimentation.

Mathematics

The measurement of skilled motor performance is a major component of physical education programs. Students are assessed using a variety of measurements, such as time (e.g., time in the 50-yard dash), distance (e.g., the broad jump), and number of successful trials (e.g., number of successful free throws out of 10 attempts). Physical education teachers can immerse students in the collection and manipulation of numeric data by requiring students to measure their own performance and compare their performance to established norms. Repeated measurements across time would enable the students to graph their performance either individually or as mean levels representing the central tendencies of performance for an entire class. Of course, statistical computer software can be used in introducing students to the use of computer technology in the analysis of data.

Students could investigate hypotheses about the variables that might contribute to motor performance. Height, weight, strength, reaction time, and percent body fat could be used in performing correlations or multiple-regression analyses on motor performance data. Predictions regarding the hypothesized influence of a myriad of variables could be supported or disproved by the findings of students' experiments.

Physical education and sport are content areas rich in statistical tradition. As mentioned previously, normative statistics are available for a number of standardized tests of motor-skill performance. In addition, virtually all sports involve the ongoing collection of performance data. Baseball is a good example. Baseball statisticians collect and analyze performance data to determine batting averages, earned run averages, slugging percentages, and fielding percentages. They also conduct more sophisticated analyses to determine trends that would assist in deciding when to call for a hit and run, a bunt, or a squeeze play. Learning activities that require the students

Diane M. Halle Library
ENDICOTT COLLEGE
Beverly, MA 01915

to collect and analyze the statistics in baseball or other popular sports assist them in understanding the relevance of mathematics in the real world. Sport education, described in chapter 2, routinely engages students in the roles of statistician and record keeper. It would be easy to extend this activity to include the types of mathematical manipulations described previously.

Language Arts

The conceptual framework provided by movement education presented in chapter 1 provides a movement vocabulary that can be used in enriching the vocabulary of young students. An added benefit is that movement education requires that students not only understand the meaning of words but also use the words to solve movement problems. The conceptual framework used in movement education was developed by Rudolf von Laban to enable dancers and choreographers to communicate with one another using a common language. Modifications of Laban's framework are used in movement education in elementary physical education; these modifications typically consist of body awareness, space, relationships, and force.

The vocabulary of movement education is extensive and provides the child with the opportunity to use movement to explore the use of skill words in the English language. Of course, the movement education concept can also easily be adapted for teaching students vocabulary in any language.

Creative use of skill verbs can also be used in reinforcing a variety of concepts taught in the classroom. Vocabulary such as *fly*, *drive*, *eat*, *sit*, *stand*, and *work* can be used to challenge the creative movement abilities of students through the use of language during physical education classes. Teachers have long lamented the difficulty of engaging students in written composition. Strategies that take advantage of students' inherent interest in sport can make writing a more attractive activity. Physical education can make a positive contribution to writing efforts across the curriculum in a variety of ways. Students could be provided with assignments to write about their favorite sport or sport hero. Also, students could be assigned to cover a sporting event and write a news article. Another possible class activity could be for the class to adopt a local athletic team and begin a correspondence project. Students could be assigned a specific player on the team with whom they would correspond on a regular basis. These and other types of writing assignments can be incorporated as an integral component of physical education units—not as a punishment for not dressing for class or other inappropriate behavior, but because writing can be used as an effective method for facilitating learning about sport and physical education.

One of the most important objectives of education is to encourage students to adopt a lifestyle that includes reading on a regular basis. The reading teacher needs to encourage this behavior by providing students with reading materials that are engaging. Given the interest that many

. M. H. illo Library
. . . LL . GE
. . . MA 01915

students have in sport, using sport-related reading materials would be an ideal way of promoting reading among students. Numerous books about sport at all academic levels can be used for engaging students in reading. Teachers can use magazines, such as *Sports Illustrated for Kids,* to encourage reading. Physical educators, in collaboration with classroom teachers and school librarians, should take the responsibility for developing a collection of age-appropriate sport-related reading materials.

Social Studies

Social studies involves the study of the characteristics of past and present civilizations. An integral part of all civilizations are the games, sport, and dance in which members of various societies engage. Throughout antiquity and in more contemporary societies, sporting events have played a major role in military preparedness (e.g., archery, javelin throwing, wrestling, running, chariot racing, jumping). Olympic-style activities conducted in the elementary school provide an ideal vehicle for exploring the cultures of antiquity.

Classes could be assigned a particular country (e.g., Sparta, Persia, Syria, Egypt, Crete) to study the culture, costumes, food, literature, recreational activities, music, and dance of a culture while students practice the sporting events they will participate in during the upcoming Olympics. On the day of the Olympics, the classes would march onto the playing fields dressed in the attire and playing music characteristic of their adopted countries. The grand entrance would be followed by the actual participation in the events of the Olympics.

Dance has a long history and played an important role in the religious ceremonies of many ancient societies. More recently, folk, social, and square dances have become important vehicles for the transmission of shared sociocultural values of most societies. These dances are used in celebrating important social events such as weddings, funerals, harvests, and historical events. Study of and participation in the types of dance created by past and current civilizations provides students with a valuable experience of the social dynamics of other cultures.

A culminating event could be a folk fair, where students perform various dances for teachers and parents. For example, in Las Cruces, New Mexico, hoedowns are a popular part of the physical education program. Students are taught a number of country-western dances (e.g, the two-step, cotton-eye Joe, and western swing) during physical education. Typically, classroom teachers simultaneously teach a unit on the history, customs, lifestyles, and other social traditions of the southwestern United States.

After the units are completed, students and parents are invited to the school to participate in an evening of country-western dance in a cafeteria that is decorated in an authentic southwestern motif. Teachers, parents, and students prepare chili, beans, enchiladas, caldillo, sopaipillas, and other traditional

Teaching the important role of dance in various cultures is a good way of integrating social studies into physical education.

examples of Southwestern cuisine that are sold to help raise funds for future educational projects. To attend the hoedown, each student must bring one parent or guardian as the price of admission. This ensures that many parents are involved in this part of the physical education curriculum.

Learning Activity 3.2

In addition to the ideas mentioned previously, describe other ways of making physical education fun for students by using integration.

Incorporate Music Into the Tasks

Teacher educators (Darst, van der Mars, & Cusimano, 1998) and curriculum developers (Rosengard, McKenzie, & Short, 2000) have advocated the inclusion of music in physical education programs. The use of popular music can add excitement to the instructional climate. Students' involvement and on-task behavior increase dramatically when music is used. In fact, students will inevitably complain if music is not available after music has been used for a period of time. Music can also provide students with choice. For example, students can be assigned to select and bring their own music or download and burn CDs for use in physical education class. This provides students with a sense of ownership regarding physical education programming and will naturally engender more active participation. Teachers can bring in "oldies" (e.g., '60s music, Motown, bubblegum) to give students a feel for what music and culture were like in previous days. Music from a variety of countries or regions can also be used in enriching the cultural experience of physical education.

Music can also be used as a management tool. Many teachers use music to start and stop activities. When the music begins, so do the students; when the music stops, the students also stop. Music that reflects different types of moods or rhythms can also be used to speed up or slow down students' level or intensity of activity.

Design Tasks That Reduce Physical and Emotional Danger

The task design principles presented thus far are ways of creating tasks and instructional climates that are interesting and fun. However, there are elements of risk, both emotional and physical, in physical education classes that can undermine the efficacy of these strategies.

Recent research indicates that emotions can play an important role in brain function and learning. Appropriate types and levels of emotional activation facilitate learning by chemically stimulating the brain. However, extremes of stress and anxiety can have a debilitating effect on brain function (Sprenger, 1999). In physical education, students are often inappropriately placed in highly stressful situations, which may cause them to cognitively withdraw from instructional activities. Following are developmentally appropriate strategies that will increase students' success and reduce stress in physical education settings.

Safe Equipment

The anxiety and stress associated with unsuccessful attempts at learning a skill can be reduced by using equipment that more closely matches the student's size and skill level. Even if there is equipment for each student, it may be too hard, large, or heavy for younger or less able students. Providing striking implements of varying lengths and balls of varying sizes and softness (Nerf balls) allows students to choose the equipment that best meets their needs. In any activity requiring equipment, several variations in size, weight, and length should be available to accommodate individual differences.

Intuitively, students will have more success if the equipment they are using will not hurt them. To decrease fear, smaller, lighter, and softer balls need to be used, particularly at the elementary level. At this level, and even with older children, Nerf balls, volleyball trainers, and other soft objects can be more appropriate than regulation-sized balls.

Safe Space

In invasion games, participants try to move an object through another team's space to a goal line or goal area. Soccer and basketball are good examples of invasion games. A problem with invasion games is that students often are not prepared to contend with opponents who try to take their ball away or block their progress downfield. As a result, players frequently lose control of objects or have objects stolen by opponents, both of which can result in feelings of failure.

A way of dealing with this problem is a strategy referred to as *safe space* (Housner, 2001). Safe space is provided by separating offensive and defensive players on the playing field with barriers such as cones or lines. The purpose of safe space is to permit players to handle objects without being confronted by an opposing player. Without opponents entering their space, students scan the field, look for an open shot or passing opportunities, and execute skills in an unhurried, less stressful manner. As students become more competent in decision making, the teacher can gradually take the boundaries away. For example, the middle boundary might be removed first, thus enabling the offensive players for each team to interact in the middle of the field. Then, as experience and skill develop, the other boundaries would be removed so that all players are free to move throughout the entire field. Of course, this can be done with the use of small-sided games before full-sided games are implemented. See figure 3.1 for a description of end ball, a game that uses the concept of safe space. End ball is also a versatile game, in that many other "safe space" games can be played using the basic structure.

Description of End Ball

A. **Objectives.** Students apply object-manipulation skills (e.g., tossing, throwing, kicking, striking, rolling) and project or strike objects past an end (goal) line and intercept and receive (e.g., trap, catch) moving objects to protect the end (goal) line. Students will demonstrate appropriate form when performing the selected skills and a thoughtful and unhurried approach to selecting and executing skills.

(continued)

Figure 3.1   Description of end ball.

Adapted, by permission, from L. Housner, 2001, "Teaching physical education with the brain in mind," *Teaching Elementary Physical Education* 12(5): 38-40.

B. **Organization.** Students are divided into two teams, As and Bs. Each team is divided into two groups: offense and defense. The field is divided into four sections with the use of three sets of cones placed between the opposing players. Offensive and defensive players are provided with **safe space** between the cones, where they can plan and perform skills without interference from opposing players. As are one team and Bs are the other. The As and Bs in the middle of the field are the offense and the As and Bs on the end (goal) lines are the defense.

G	A	C	B	C	A	C	B	G
O	A	O	B	O	A	O	B	O
A	A	N	B	N	A	N	B	A
L	A	E	B	E	A	E	B	L
		S		S		S		

C. **Equipment.** Students use objects to toss, kick, roll, strike, and pass toward the end (goal) line. (Note: Nerf balls or soft objects should be used because defenders will try to intercept the objects.)

D. **Description.** Students on offense project or deflect objects across the end line. A point is scored if an object crosses the end line. If students on defense intercept the objects, they project or deflect the objects over or through the opposing offense to their offensive teammates, who then project or deflect objects past the other end line.

E. **Variations.** Different object manipulation skills (e.g., throw, roll, kick, strike) can be used. Different objects (e.g., Frisbees, utility balls, tennis balls) can be used. The number of objects can be varied to speed up or slow down the activity. Pins can be set up along the end line, and the objective would be to knock down the pins to earn points.

F. **Things to look for.** Do the children aim before trying to score? Do the players work together by passing back and forth? Do players think strategically by looking for open spaces in the opposing formations? Do players take advantage of safe space by taking time to carefully plan shots and sometimes faking shots and then passing to move opponents out of position?

Figure 3.1   *(continued)*

Emotional Safety

The instructional climate that teachers establish can have a dramatic effect on the interest and motivation of students. Researchers (Mitchell, 1996; Solmon, 1996; Xiang & Lee, 1998) have found that a mastery-oriented climate characterized by the effortful completion of tasks and achievement of self-competence without concern for comparisons with fellow students can increase students' intrinsic motivation, willingness to choose demanding tasks, enjoyment, and acceptance of responsibility for successes and failures. Performance-oriented climates emphasize demonstrating ability superior to that of other students and can engender attribution of success and failure to ability. In a performance-oriented climate, children are less willing to attempt challenging tasks.

A popular technique for creating a mastery climate is referred to as the TARGET approach (Alderman, Beighle, & Pangrazi, 2006; Morgan & Carpenter, 2002). TARGET is an acronym for task, authority, recognition, grouping, evaluation, and time, which are the six dimensions for creating a mastery climate. The **task dimension** should be used when designing tasks that are varied, interesting, and challenging. For the **authority dimension,** students are provided with opportunities to make decisions or choices. **Recognition** should be given to students for improving and putting forth a strong effort. The **grouping dimension** is used in creating cooperative groups that are composed of students of varied abilities. **Evaluation** should be focused on improvement and effort and delivered in privacy. Finally, adequate **time** should be made available for students to progress in an optimal and individualized manner.

Recently, researchers (Chelladurai, 2005) have argued that to achieve optimal athletic performance, it may be appropriate to combine a mastery approach with a performance-oriented approach. In this way athletes would apply a mastery approach when practicing, learning new skills, and preparing for competition, and would apply a performance approach when competing for a position on the team and then, ultimately, competing to achieve success by besting opponents. In an athletic context, it makes sense to create climates that enable athletes to compete against themselves to achieve as much as their potential and effort allow, while simultaneously competing against opponents with the goal of winning. Of course, in youth sport and physical education classes where students are primarily learning and applying new skills, emphasizing a mastery orientation would be the most developmentally appropriate approach. The goal in these settings is to assist students in achieving competence and, therefore, becoming skillful enough to enjoy competition.

Learning Activity 3.3

Read the article "Enhancing Motivation in Physical Education" (Alderman, Beighle, & Pangrazi, 2006). Then, on your own or in small groups, pick a fundamental or sport skill and create a practice or lesson plan applying the TARGET approach to creating a mastery climate.

Summary

Interesting tasks will engender higher levels of activity, both physical and cognitive, than boring tasks. A number of techniques for making tasks more interesting and engaging for children are provided in this chapter. Incorporating variety, goals, inherent feedback, choice, and music into instructional tasks can make tasks more interesting. Integrating academic content into tasks can also increase the interest level of students. Finally, physical and emotional safety is an important element in making tasks engaging rather than intimidating; several strategies to make lessons safe are described.

Design Tasks That Stimulate Cognitive Engagement

Research on teaching, particularly in the area of classroom research, has moved beyond time on task and embraced the role of students' cognition in learning. Research indicates that students mediate instruction by constructing meaning, cognitively and socially, as they interact with classroom tasks (Doyle, 1986). Promoting learners' cognitive engagement, either through direct instruction or the provision of tasks that elicit appropriate strategies or representations, can promote learning. In an early meta-analysis, Wang, Haertel, and Walberg (1990) provide evidence indicating that students' use of effective cognitive-processing strategies are more highly related to school learning than typically powerful predictors such as characteristics of the community, school, and classroom. More recently, in another meta-analysis, Marzano, Pickering, and Pollock (2001) found that instructional strategies that stimulate student cognition are the most effective in terms of facilitating achievement. The following eight categories, listed in order beginning with the highest effect size, were found to be the most effective:

1. Identifying similarities and differences
2. Summarizing and note taking
3. Reinforcing effort and providing recognition
4. Engaging in homework and practice
5. Using nonlinguistic representations
6. Setting objectives and providing feedback
7. Generating and testing hypotheses
8. Using questions, cues, and advanced organizers

Researchers in sport and physical education have begun to acknowledge the importance of the role of cognition in learning (Solmon & Lee, 1992; Rink, 2002). In this chapter, strategies for activating cognitive engagement in sport and physical education are presented. Upon completion of this chapter, the teacher should be able to do the following:

1. Clearly explain and demonstrate the skill or task.
2. Use cues to stimulate students' thinking.
3. Check for students' understanding.
4. Use questioning to extend students' thinking.
5. Incorporate cognitive strategies in tasks.
6. Provide students with direct instruction on thinking skills.

Clearly Explain and Demonstrate Skills and Tasks

Research on teaching has uncovered several variables of teachers' behavior that are associated with students' learning. These variables have been organized into a model of teaching called direct instruction. An important component of direct instruction is presenting tasks to students. It is important that new content be presented with clarity. Students should be provided with demonstrations and explanations that clearly indicate what is being taught, why it is being taught, and how the students can learn what is being taught. In the area of physical education, Rink and Werner (1989) developed an observation instrument referred to as the Qualitative Measures of Teaching Performance Scale (QMTPS), which is based on findings of direct instruction, motor learning research on demonstrations and instructional cues, and information-processing theory that also emphasizes the importance of providing clear demonstrations and explanations. The QMTPS is composed of the following seven categories:

1. Clarity
2. Demonstration
3. Number of instructional cues
4. Accuracy of cues
5. Quality of instructional cues
6. Appropriateness of students' responses
7. Feedback

The QMTPS has been found to be related to effective skill teaching and learning in physical education settings (Rink, 1996). The following guidelines should assist the teacher in providing clear demonstrations and explanations.

State the Objective

Stating the objective helps students understand the content of the lesson before teaching begins. Stating the objective provides an overview of lesson or unit content and the specific objectives that will be addressed during the lesson. In physical education, lesson objectives should be based on National Association for Sport and Physical Education (NASPE) standards. According to the definition developed by NASPE (1992), a physically educated person *has* skills, *is* physically fit, *does* participate in regular physical activity, *knows* the benefits of physical activity, and *values* physical activity. These areas are delineated in figure 4.1.

A physically educated person . . .

Has **learned skills necessary to perform a variety of physical activities.**

1. Moves using concepts of body awareness, spatial awareness, effort, and relationships.
2. Demonstrates competence in a variety of manipulative, locomotor, and nonlocomotor skills.
3. Demonstrates competence in combinations of manipulative, locomotor, and nonlocomotor skills performed individually and with others.
4. Demonstrates competence in many different forms of physical activity.
5. Demonstrates proficiency in a few forms of physical activity.
6. Has learned how to learn new skills.

Is **physically fit.**

7. Assesses, achieves, and maintains physical fitness.
8. Designs safe, personal fitness programs in accordance with principles of training and conditioning.

Does **participate regularly in physical activity.**

9. Participates in health-enhancing physical activity at least three times a week.
10. Selects and regularly participates in lifetime physical activities.

(continued)

Figure 4.1   Definition of the physically educated person outcomes of quality physical education programs.

Outcomes of Quality Physical Education Programs (1992) adapted with permission from the National Association for Sport and Physical Education (NASPE), 1900 Association Drive, Reston, VA 20191-1599.

Knows **the implications and benefits of involvement in physical activities.**

11. Identifies the benefits, costs, and obligations associated with regular participation in physical activity.

12. Recognizes the risk and safety factors associated with regular participation in physical activity.

13. Applies concepts and principles to the development of motor skills.

14. Understands that wellness involves more than being physically fit.

15. Knows the rules, strategies, and appropriate behaviors for selected physical activities.

16. Recognizes that participation in physical activity can lead to multicultural and international understanding.

17. Understands that physical activity provides the opportunity for enjoyment, self-expression, and communication.

Values **physical activity and its contributions to a healthful lifestyle.**

18. Appreciates the relationships with others that result from participation in physical activity.

19. Respects the role that regular physical activity plays in the pursuit of lifelong health and well-being.

20. Cherishes the feelings that result from regular participation in physical activity.

Figure 4.1 *(continued)*

Many state departments of education have adopted the NASPE standards and expanded them to define the outcomes associated with quality K-12 physical education programs. These outcomes represent the content that should be shared with students when stating the objectives on units and lessons. The following are several strategies that can be used when stating the objective.

• **Graphic organizers.** When stating the objective, using a graphic organizer that pictorially represents the content can assist students in organizing content in memory (figure 4.2). Concept maps capture large amounts of information in a single visual representation and can be used for many types of information. For example, conceptual maps that display the content of a unit, the sequence of instruction, and the relationships between these aspects of the unit can be presented, or students can draw their own conceptual maps (Scantling, McAleese, Tietjen, & Strand, 1992). Mapping tasks can increase the students' attention to the instructional activities of lessons and practice sessions and facilitate the organization of information in memory.

Vickers (1990) has proposed that employing expert knowledge structures may be an effective guide for curriculum development in sport and physical

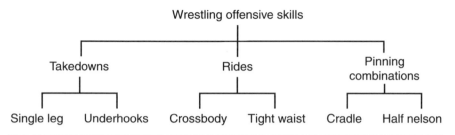

Figure 4.2   Graphic organizer for offensive skills in wrestling.

education. This assumption formed the foundation of the Human Kinetics *Steps to Success Activity Series* (1990), in which expert knowledge structures were used as graphic or pictorial frameworks for instructional programs in archery, bowling, golf, tennis, volleyball, and other sports.

- **Pre- and postlesson questions and objectives.** Stating the objectives that students will achieve or indicating the questions that students should be able to answer before or after instruction lets students know in advance what they will do in class. Objectives and questions can be provided verbally as part of the introduction of a unit or lesson, or they can be presented visually by placing them on bulletin or chalk boards, at stations, or directly on task sheets. By letting students know what to expect, they will be cognitively prepared when new information is provided and attention will also be increased. Of course, as attentiveness increases, so will the retention of information.

- **Highlighting similarities.** Linking skills that are similar or can be transferred from one sporting situation to another can be useful in facilitating learning. For example, students should be made aware that the overarm throwing motion is used in many sport skills, such as the badminton smash and overhead clear, tennis serve and smash, volleyball serve and spike, javelin throw, and ceiling shot in racquetball. Students who are made aware of the similarities between overarm skills that are performed in different sport contexts should positively transfer that knowledge between sport contexts. Some skills are similar conceptually rather than in form. For example, the crossover dribble, whether in basketball, soccer, or field hockey, is designed to place the dribbler's body between the defender and the ball. Assisting students in learning relationships and similarities between how skills are performed and applied can assist in transferring skills from one sport to another.

Provide a Motivational Set

Providing a motivational set is different from stating the objective because it explains to the students why the activities are important and meaningful to them. The relevance and value of learning content in physical education are substantial and need to be shared with students. Also, providing a motivational set will contribute to obtaining and maintaining students' attention.

- **Fitness and health.** Sport and physical education provide opportunities for students to achieve increased levels of fitness. Students should be taught about the long- and short-term health benefits of engaging in regular physical activity. Students also should know about the serious health problems (e.g., obesity, type 2 diabetes, heart disease) associated with lack of physical activity.

- **Fun and success.** Students should know about the fun associated with playing sport and that physical education will teach them the skills they need in order to play the games. Students should be informed that they will get to play fun lead-up tasks and games; eventually, when they have achieved success in these tasks, they will play the game.

- **Social interaction.** Students should be reminded that they rarely get the opportunity to play with classmates. For many students, social interaction is a primary reason for engaging in physical education and physical activity (Weiss, 2000); Goodlad (1984) points out that physical education is characterized by less passive seatwork and more active learning than academic subjects involve. Teachers need to take advantage of this unique quality and make sure that students understand that this is another reason why sport, physical education, and physical activity are fun.

- **Transfer.** Students should be informed that what they learn will transfer to other sports and physical activities. They should understand that the skills they will learn, the strategies they will learn, and the fitness they will achieve applies to other sports and physical activities.

Learning Activity 4.1

List and describe other ways of explaining why physical education is relevant for students.

Demonstrate

After stating the objective (what) and providing a motivational set (why), the teacher typically will explain and demonstrate how to do the skills to be performed. An important way of focusing students' attention on the key elements of a skill is to show the students how the skills are to be performed. As the saying goes, "A picture is worth a thousand words."

Research provides several guidelines for maximizing the effectiveness of demonstrations (Housner, 1984; McCullagh, 1994). For example, when giving an explanation or demonstration, students should be arranged so they can see and hear the teacher. One way of doing this is to place students in a semi-circle, which is a formation that enables students to attend to the demonstration. Teachers should consider the position of the sun and other factors

Providing slow-motion demonstrations can help the learners remember how to perform the skill.

that might distract students. For example, they should not have students face the sun or be in a position where they can observe another class.

It can be beneficial to repeat demonstrations several times, provide slow-motion demonstrations, and break complex skills into parts for demonstration before modeling the entire skill, particularly if the parts are not interdependent. These strategies will assist students in coding the key elements of the skill and retaining the information incorporated in the demonstration.

Orienting the demonstration so that students see the demonstration from the same perspective as they will perform the skill can facilitate retention. This is why dance studios have mirrors. Using mirrors, the teacher can orient demonstrations so that the students don't have to mentally rotate the image, and at the same time the teacher can see the students' reflected images and provide feedback.

Finally, incorporating verbal descriptions or cues that point out the key elements of the skill can assist students in learning and retaining skills. The following section explores the use of cues to stimulate students' cognitive involvement in the skill-learning process.

Use Cues to Stimulate Students' Thinking*

As mentioned in chapter 1, instructional cues can be used in focusing students' attention on the critical elements of tasks. However, instructional cues

---

*The cues discussed on pages 84-90 are adapted, by permission, from L.D. Housner and D.C. Griffey, 1994, "Wax on, wax off: Pedagogical content knowledge in motor skill instruction," *Journal of Physical Education, Recreation & Dance* 65(2): 63-68.

can also be used in focusing students' attention on the cognitive elements of tasks, such as mechanical principles and strategies associated with correct applications of motor skills in game-like settings. The framework derived from Housner and Griffey (1994) and presented in table 4.1 involves two components: information processing and instructional cues. The information-processing component is based on models of skill acquisition popularized by motor learning researchers (Anshel, 1990; Gentile, 1972). These models view learners as actively engaged in the skill-learning process as they sort, interpret, and respond to large amounts of information during the skill-acquisition processes.

Information-processing theories assume that learning sport skills takes place in the following sequential stages. The student

1. understands the purpose or goal of the skill;

2. selectively attends to the environmental stimuli that is relevant for achieving the goal while at the same time ignoring stimuli irrelevant to successful completion of the goal;

3. labels and attaches meaning to the relevant stimuli by applying perceptual processes;

4. decides on a course of action that will achieve the goal and formulates a plan for a motor response;

5. organizes and initiates the selected motor response and evaluates the success of the response by interpreting available feedback;

6. modifies the next response to better achieve the goal or attempts to repeat the motor skill performed on the previous successful trial; and

7. stores the information available from the above stages in short- or long-term memory.

Stored information will influence the subsequent processing of information. As the student gains knowledge in a particular area of sport or physical activity, this knowledge assists the student to more effectively process information. Metacognition is defined as the direct, conscious control of one's own cognitive processes. With experience, students become able to use knowledge to more reflectively plan, execute, evaluate, and modify skills.

The second component of the framework is based on the assumption that teachers play an important role in assisting students to efficiently process information during skill learning and performance. Teachers use a variety of instructional cues to focus students' attention on pertinent information processes during teaching. The instructional cues described in the following text were identified in studies on the ways that expert teachers and coaches convey knowledge to students (Griffey, Housner, & Williams, 1985; Housner & Griffey, 1994).

Table 4.1   Framework for Stimulating Information Processing Using Instructional Cues

Information processing	INSTRUCTIONAL CUES			
	Verbal	Visual	Kinesthetic/ tactile	Task
1. Goal formation: What is the goal?				
2. Selective attention: What stimuli do I attend to?				
3. Perception: What do the stimuli mean?				
4. Motor plan: What response will I make?				
5. Response organization: How will I move to achieve the goal?				
6. Interpreting feedback: Did I achieve the goal?				
7. Next response: Do I move the same way or change?				
8. Information storage: What do I need to remember?				
9. Metacognition: Is everything going OK?				

Expert teachers and coaches use a variety of cues when focusing learners' attention on the various stages of information processes. Specifically, verbal, visual, kinesthetic, and task structure cues are employed when experts convey content knowledge to students.

Verbal cues are explanations, analogies or metaphors, alphanumeric labels, and other forms of verbal communication that teachers use to convey content knowledge to students. Visual cues are used to direct the student's visual system to relevant stimuli and includes live or videotaped demonstrations, graphic representations such as pictures or charts, and visual stimuli (placed on objects, the floor, and so on) that serve as targets. Kinesthetic/tactile cues are used primarily to guide the student to reproduce a desired motor pattern. Manual guidance (touching or moving the learner) or mechanical guidance (in which objects or apparatus are used to physically constrain movements) are two popular methods used by teachers. Finally, task structure cues are instructional activities and tasks used by coaches and teachers to present content to learners. Task cues include any task structure that cognitively focuses students during lessons or practice.

Examples of instructional cues are presented in the following sections. It should be noted that cues often focus students' attention on more than one stage of information processing. The examples that follow are organized according to the stage of information processing most directly engaged by the cue.

Goal of the Skill

Communicating the goal of the skill to students is critical. Students need to know whether the objective of the skill is to achieve an outcome (e.g., hit a home run), move in a certain way by using a particular form, or both. Visual demonstrations are effective for form-specific skills. Demonstrations combined with verbal labeling of the critical elements will facilitate retention. Analogies and metaphors can also be used in conveying proper form to students. In swimming, for example, a teacher could describe the movement of the arms in the breaststroke as shaped like an inverted heart.

Masser (1993) completed a study of the use of instructional cues in teaching form-specific gymnastics skills to students. Providing students with the verbal cues "Shoulders over your knuckles" for the handstand and "Forehead on your knees" or "Make yourself into a tight ball" for the forward roll resulted in significantly better performance than for students who practiced without using cues.

Even for outcome-specific skills that are closed, teachers often provide cues that assist learners in using correct form as a goal. Expert coaches and teachers manually guide students through movements to illustrate the proper motor pattern or touch students to indicate the proper positioning of a body segment. The "golfer's groove" is a mechanical device used as an aid in learning the form of the drive in golf. Students are placed inside a tubular framework and place the head of the driver against the framework. If students swing the club while maintaining contact with the framework, they will be provided with a kinesthetic representation of the ideal swing (Skrinar & Hoffman, 1978; Yost, Strauss, & Davis, 1976).

Gentile (1972) suggests that care must be taken when conveying movement goals to learners so that they do not fall victim to goal confusion. That is, students should not think that the goal of the skill is to move like the teacher. Within reason, the teacher's role is to encourage students to explore the possibilities of solving movement problems by using a variety of movement processes that will effectively achieve the outcome. Without this type of flexibility in the teaching process, the Fosbury flop and other innovations in sport might not have evolved.

Selective Attention

A popular verbal cue for focusing student attention on the ball in tennis is the bounce-hit technique (Gallwey, 1974). When performing a return of the tennis ball, it requires tennis players to say out loud "Bounce" as the tennis ball hits the surface of the court and "Hit" when the ball contacts the racket face. This focuses the players' attention on visually tracking the moving ball, moving to the correct location on the court to intercept the ball, and coordinating the swing of the racket to hit the ball. This is done without the lengthy and potentially distracting verbal descriptions of form (e.g., stance, pivot, swing, follow-through) that often accompany teaching tennis strokes.

Expert teachers use visual cues to focus students' attention selectively on the relevant stimuli related to successful performance of skills. For example, instead of repeating, "Keep your eye on the ball," experienced teachers place visible targets (e.g., Xs, faces, or numbers) on objects to facilitate the interception of stationary and moving objects for the purpose of kicking, catching, or striking. Another example would be how football coaches often place numbers on the end of footballs. The receivers are then required to yell out the number of the ball they are receiving while it is still in the air, thus facilitating visual attention to the ball.

Perception

Perception is the process of recognizing, labeling, and attaching meaning to stimuli or events. It involves learning the perceptual language of a sport in order to predict how events will typically unfold. For instance, in football if a defensive lineman moves into an upright position upon the snap of the ball, defensive players are taught to instantaneously recognize this as a pass play. Also, in racquetball when a player moves to one side of the service area and angles his or her feet toward the front corner, the experienced player will recognize this as a Z serve. As a player gains experience, he or she not only will recognize the type of serve but will also be able to predict the trajectory of the ball and the likely area where the ball will end up.

The teacher's role is to assist the learner in identifying the various types of stimuli and events that naturally occur during competition and to structure tasks so that learners will experience each and begin the process of recognizing, labeling, and attaching meaning to stimuli and events. Questioning students and having students identify and state the type of event that they expect to occur or predict the events that they hypothesize will take place can encourage them to be more cognitively engaged in the learning process. For example, football coaches have linebackers yell out "Pass" when they recognize that a pass play is being run.

Decision Making

Coaches often question athletes to encourage the rehearsal of possible upcoming strategic decisions. For example, baseball coaches have students ask themselves the question "Where will I throw the ball if it comes to me?" each time a batter comes to the plate. When the ball does come to the student, the appropriate decision has already been rehearsed and the speed of execution will be increased. Having students mentally practice strategic decisions in a variety of situations will prepare students to more effectively respond to the situation when it is actually encountered. These types of decisions are often referred to as *if–then statements* or *production systems.* Examples of if–then statements in wrestling are "If double leg, then sprawl" and "If single leg, then whizzer." Production systems are part of the strategic element of all sports, and teachers should share them with students.

The "big man" drill in basketball is used to prepare an offensive player for playing against a big center. Arm pads or brooms are used to extend the length of a defending player's reach in order to simulate a tall center. The offensive player's task is to dribble down the lane and take a jump shot, hook shot, or layup while adjusting to the "big man" who is placed in front of the basket. This helps the offensive player to make rapid adjustment decisions similar to those required when playing against a "big man" in actual game situations.

A similar task structure in football is designed to have the quarterback practice throwing over and between the outstretched arms of defensive linemen. In this task, the arms of defensive linemen are simulated by a wooden structure (six sets of two two-by-fours extending upward to a height of 8 to 10 feet [about 2.4 to 3 meters] represent the outstretched arms of oncoming defensive linemen). The quarterback's task is to take the snap, drop back into the pocket, and accurately throw the ball over and between the "arms" of linemen.

Formulating the Motor Plan

Verbal analogies and metaphors are used in many sport domains to assist the learner in formulating an effective motor plan. For example, the arm movements in the volleyball spike are described as being like drawing back the arm when shooting a bow and arrow.

In golf, teachers use a clock analogy to establish the relationship between the goals of different types of shots and the length of the swing. Students visualize a large clock behind them, with 12:00 at their head and 6:00 at their feet. The swing length for various shots is represented by the distance between two times on the clock. For example, when chipping, the backswing would begin at 7:00 for short distances (15 to 20 yards, or about

14 to 18 meters), at 8:00 for moderate distances (20 to 40 yards, or about 18 to 36 meters), and at 9:00 for longer distances (40 to 60 yards, or about 36 to 55 meters).

Kinesthetic/tactile cues are used to assist the student in formulating a motor plan that reflects the proper positioning or sequencing of body segments. For instance, golf instructors will place a golf ball under the right arm of the student in order to emphasize keeping the right arm close to the body during the swing. Placing a golf ball under the outside part of the right foot enables the student to vividly feel the weight shift.

Springboard diving instructors foster a high arc in divers by placing a rope approximately 1 foot (30 cm) in front of the end of the board at chest height. The rope provides a concrete obstacle that the diver must clear. Of course, this forces the diver to increase the height of the dive. A similar cue has been used by football coaches to ensure that an offensive lineman stays low during the first few steps of the block. Metal blocking chutes are designed to create a tunnel through which the lineman can run only by staying low. Finally, track coaches sometimes will place a rope a few feet in front of the sprinter and about waist high to force the runner to stay low when coming out of the blocks.

Torbert (1982) has suggested a way of emphasizing the level swing in batting. In the task, three balls are placed on three batting tees placed in a straight line. The task is to swing so that contact is made with all three balls with a single swing. To accomplish this, the batter must swing level so that the bat hits "through" the balls.

Interpreting Available Feedback and the Next Response

Placing a poster next to an accuracy task that asks students, "Did the ball hit the target and, if so, where? What will you do on your next throw? Do you need to throw higher or lower, softer or harder, to the left or right?" can assist students in interpreting feedback and planning the next response. Setting up a station where students can videotape and analyze their skill performance can be a productive way to encourage students to be mindful movers and think about how they are trying to solve the movement problem. Having students set goals for improving skills that focus on both the form and the outcome of skills can facilitate students' use of feedback and planning for their next responses.

Reciprocal teaching can be an effective way to assist students in thinking about the meaning of feedback and how to modify responses to improve performance. Students placed in the role of observer and feedback agent can be assigned the additional task of assisting the learner in planning the next response.

Information Storage

Letters, numbers, or simple words can be used to enhance students' retention of the correct sequence of movements in a skill. For example, in dance, teachers use many simple labels to assist students in learning and remembering dance steps. For example, the two-step is often represented by the verbal label "slow, slow–fast, fast." Most skills can be analyzed into discrete steps or sequences of movements that can then be assigned labels to facilitate retention. The form of the free throw in basketball is often recalled using the acronym BEEF, which represents the following:

B = Balance. Go on the foul line, get balanced and steady in your stance.

E = Eyes. Look at the back or the front of the rim.

E = Elbow. Your elbow should be in line with the basketball hoop.

F = Follow through. Make sure you follow through with the hand staying up in a gooseneck position and thumb pointing at your feet.

Making associations between prior knowledge and new information can also facilitate retention. Informing the student that the skill to be learned (e.g., a tennis serve) is similar to a skill already learned (e.g., overhand throw) can assist the learner in assimilating new information into memory.

Attaching a visual image with a verbal label can enhance memory by providing two codes for retaining information (Paivio, 1971). Analogies or metaphors often have vivid images as part of the verbal label (for example, the arm motion in the sidestroke in swimming is frequently described as picking an apple and placing it in the other hand, which places it in a basket; the arm motion in bowling is like a pendulum; and the arm position in the overhand throw begins in the shape of an "L"). Finally, in tennis, the backhand is described as like drawing a sword from a sheath and the back-scratch position is used to describe the position of the racket during the serve. Analogies and metaphors with verbal labels and vivid visual images are easier to remember because two codes are available for coding and retrieving the information.

Metacognition

Teachers use verbal cues to engage metacognitive processes in learners. For example, questioning strategies can be used to focus students' attention on the overall game strategy during competitive play. In many sports, players can be asked to summarize the strengths and weaknesses of their opponents in the current contest or to verbally evaluate their own performances. During timeouts or between innings, games, holes, and the like, players can be challenged to identify the shots or strategies that they used, and to determine whether they are successful and need to be maintained or if they are unsuccessful and need to be modified.

Learning Activity 4.2

Interview a coach, find out what instructional cues he or she uses in coaching the sport, and classify the cues according to the framework in table 4.1 (on page 83).

Check for Students' Understanding

Comprehension monitoring, known as checks for understanding (CFU), has been consistently related to learning in classroom contexts (Rosenshine & Stevens, 1986; Wittrock, 1991). CFU has been a significant instructional component of direct instruction (Rink, 2002). In a recent study conducted at West Virginia University (Ayers et al., 2005), students who received CFU added significantly more critical elements to their standing broad jump performance and recalled more of the critical elements (92%) than students who received only practice (8%) or demonstration and cueing followed by practice (66%).

The first step in using CFU is establishing a list of the critical elements (things to look for), including the progression toward a mature movement pattern and common errors that one might expect to encounter when teaching specific skills. The teacher should also create a list of cognitive and affective objectives that should be reflected in students' learning, such as an understanding of health-related fitness principles, mechanical principles, instructional cues, strategic concepts, and teamwork.

Once the teacher knows what to look for, he or she needs to assume a position that enables the observation of as many students as possible, to determine which students need assistance. An effective teacher can be involved with providing individuals with instruction while simultaneously observing the rest of the students. The following are several techniques for checking comprehension.

• **Questioning.** This is the most straightforward and probably the most frequently used technique for CFU. However, most questions used by teachers are low-level recall questions that require little thinking on the part of students. When asking questions, the teacher should plan the questioning strategy in advance so that it will challenge students. Johnson (1997) provides several suggestions for making questioning a more productive and thoughtful part of teaching. The following is a list of these and other suggestions, obtained from the Maryland State Department of Education.

1. Prompt *how* questions are to be answered. For example, say, "Raise your hand to answer the following question." This prompts students not to call out answers, which robs students of processing the question and deciding on an answer.

2. Provide at least 5 seconds of time after a question or a response so that students will have time to think about the question and search their memories for an answer. This allows students to critically analyze the question posed.

3. If there are several components to the question, such as the number of critical elements for a skill or the number of food groups, ask several students to supply one component. This keeps students' attention because any student could be called on to contribute to the answer.

4. Ask follow-up questions, such as "How? Why do you know? Can you give me an example? Can you tell me more?" so that students are required to process information more deeply and justify their answers.

5. Ask open-ended questions so that students understand that often there is more than one correct answer and that it is important to consider alternatives. A question such as "Do you need to bend your knees in order to jump?" evokes a one-word answer. But an open-ended question such as "Describe what you need to do when you jump" encourages a child to describe the elements involved in the skill.

6. Use "think–pair–share" when asking questions. After the question, allow some time for students to think on their own, then have them share their ideas with a partner, and then have a group discussion.

7. Call on students randomly so that they understand that you will sometimes call on those who do not raise their hands.

8. Ask students to "unpack their thinking" by having them describe how they came to their conclusions.

9. Ask for a summary to encourage active listening.

10. When questioning, play devil's advocate by requiring students to defend their thinking against other points of view.

11. Allow students to call on other students to answer questions.

12. Encourage questioning by providing opportunities for students to generate their own questions.

13. If students have difficulty answering questions, don't forget that it is acceptable for the teacher to cue or give hints to the students.

From Maryland State Department of Education

Using the technique of questioning to check for students' understanding should be planned in advance so that the questioning challenges the students in numerous ways.

• **Choral response.** The teacher can assess the entire class using choral responses from students. The teacher simply asks a question and the students all answer in unison when the teacher gives a signal. If the teacher hears mumbling or a cacophony of responses, then it would be apparent that the students as a whole do not know the answer. If, on the other hand, the group gives a group response that is in unison and easily understood, then it would be apparent that most students understand. A similar technique is called a *poker chip survey* (Graham, 2001). The teacher poses a question and each student responds by placing a red poker chip in a box if the answer is yes or black if it is no. Checking the distribution of the chips gives a quick glimpse into the level of understanding of the class. An easier class survey is to have students give a thumbs-up (yes) or a thumbs-down (no) in response to a question.

• **Guided practice.** After the subject matter, such as dribbling a basketball, has been presented, students can be required to dribble all together. The teacher can quickly scan the class while the students are dribbling and determine whether they can dribble adequately. Complex skills can be broken down into components for guided practice. For example, a teacher may ask students to demonstrate a balanced stance for the free throw in basketball (B), then the position of the elbow and eyes (EE), and finally the follow-through (F) separately, and then in combination, when applying the BEEF strategy to the free throw.

- **Students' explanations.** In this technique, the teacher asks the students to explain or demonstrate the content to a classmate or teammate. Students' explanations may also include guiding a partner through a motor skill; recalling and explaining teaching cues presented; and explaining the meaning of a concept, principle, rule, or strategy. As the students explain, the teacher should walk around and observe for correct responses.

- **Homework.** Having learners perform cognitive, psychomotor, or fitness tasks at home can be an effective way of using CFU without taking up valuable class time. Children should be physically active during class, and homework is an ideal way of using CFU outside of class. There are also several advantages to using homework in this way. First, it sends a message home that physical education is a subject matter of substance and that it needs to be taken seriously. Second, it can be used to involve parents in students' physical education. Ideally, some homework tasks may require the active participation of the family and, as indicated earlier, one goal of physical education is to enhance the activity levels of students and their families outside of class. Finally, for students who have access to a computer and the Internet, homework is an ideal way to integrate technology into the curriculum. Students could search the Web for health-related fitness information or create and maintain a daily journal focusing on personal fitness or skill development. The journal could then be submitted via e-mail to the teacher or organized into a class newsletter.

Use Questioning to Extend Students' Thinking

When questioning students, teachers need to require more than simple recall. While recall of facts is important, teachers should actively and systematically plan to extend students' thinking by asking questions that move beyond recall. The following list (obtained from the Maryland State Department of Education) is a hierarchy of questions based on Bloom's taxonomy that teachers can use to extend students' thinking. Teachers can use this classification system to evaluate their own questioning behavior and determine whether they are relying on only lower-level recall questions or are engaging students cognitively through the use of increasingly challenging questions.

1. Recall questions: Ask students who, what, when, where, and why.
2. Comparison questions: How is _____ similar to or different from _____?
3. Identifying attributes: What are the characteristics or parts of _____?
4. Classifying questions: How might you classify _____ into categories?

5. Ordering questions: Arrange _____ into a sequence according to _____.

6. Identifying relationships and patterns: Create an outline, diagram, or web of _____.

7. Representing: What other ways might we show or illustrate _____?

8. Identifying main ideas: What is the key concept in _____? Restate the main idea of _____ in your own words.

9. Identifying errors: What's wrong with _____?

10. Inferring: What can you infer from _____? What conclusions can be drawn from _____?

11. Predicting: What might happen if _____?

12. Elaborating: What ideas or details can you add to _____? Give an example of _____.

13. Summarizing: Can you summarize _____?

14. Establishing criteria: What criteria would you use to judge or evaluate _____?

15. Verifying: What evidence supports _____? How might we confirm or disconfirm _____?

From Maryland State Department of Education

Teachers can encourage critical thinking by asking questions that require students to think beyond the recall of facts. Using the previous classifications, the teacher can challenge students to engage cognitively in sport and physical activities. Application questions such as "When do you think you would use the crossover dribble in field hockey or basketball?" or evaluation questions such as "Why does a football receiver who uses feinting or faking have an advantage?" or "Why does stepping with opposition help you throw harder?" can stimulate students to think more deeply and, therefore, understand and retain information better.

Incorporate Cognitive Strategies in Tasks

Designing tasks that incorporate or elicit cognitive engagement in students can facilitate students' attention, learning, and retention. The following are several ways to encourage students' cognitive engagement through task design.

Cue and Strategy Reminders

The teacher can incorporate cue reminders in tasks so that students will not forget the cues that were provided in the introduction of the lesson. For example, the teacher can place verbal cues or pictures on task sheets or station cards to remind students to think about the cues.

Singer (1988; 1990) developed and validated the use of a five-step strategy for learning closed skills. The strategy is derived from information-processing models of skill acquisition and consolidates the cognitive strategies that underlie skill learning into five simple steps. These steps can be used in the direct instruction of strategies or placed on posters or bulletin boards in the gym or at stations so students are reminded to use the strategy. Of course, both direct instruction and incorporating the strategies as part of task design can be used.

> Step 1: Ready. Get comfortable physically, attain an optimal mental and emotional state, and do things in preparation that are associated with previous best performances. Be consistent in attaining the preparatory state for the act.
>
> Step 2: Image. Mentally picture yourself performing the act. Think positive and feel confident. Feel the movement.
>
> Step 3: Focus. Concentrate intensely on one relevant feature and think only of this cue. Block out all other thoughts.
>
> Step 4: Execute. Do it. Do not think of anything about the act itself or the possible outcome.
>
> Step 5: Evaluate. Use available feedback information to learn from. Assess the performance outcome and the effectiveness of each step in the routine and adjust any procedure next time, if needed.

Like reminders for cues, verbal cues on task sheets or station cards could be used for reminding students about the steps in the five-step strategy.

Contextual Interference

Research on contextual interference has found that providing varying practice conditions will facilitate the retention of motor skills (Magill, 2004; Magill & Hall, 1990). For example, when teaching a basketball lesson, having students rotate to free-throw, layup, dribbling, and passing stations will facilitate better skill retention than practicing dribbling for the entire lesson. The hypothesis put forth for this phenomenon is that students are forced to switch and refocus attention when new tasks are confronted. This increased cognitive level of processing ostensibly leads to greater retention. The teacher or coach can integrate contextual interference into practice sessions to assist students in becoming more engaged cognitively.

Tactical Tasks

Teachers want their students to be effective decision makers when playing games, and creative teachers can provide instructional tasks that illuminate key tactical concepts. As mentioned in chapter 2, Griffin, Mitchell, and Oslin (1997) have characterized games as belonging to four basic categories: invasion (e.g., basketball, soccer, lacrosse), net or wall (e.g., tennis, badminton, racquetball), fielding or run scoring (e.g., baseball, cricket), and target (e.g., golf, bowling). Each of these types of games has different tactics, and even within categories there may be tactics that are unique to various games. Some examples of tactics for invasion games are listed in table 2.2 (see page 53).

Critical-Thinking Tasks

McBride (1995) has argued that teachers need to focus on assisting students to think more effectively. Critical thinking is an elusive concept and has been defined as reflective decision making (McBride & Cleland, 1998), creative problem solving (Tishman & Perkins, 1995), or a persistent and curious disposition toward inquiry (Blitzer, 1995). Regardless of the definition adopted, a central tenet of critical thinking is to engage students in the conscious and reflective application of higher-order intellectual processes such as applying, comparing, evaluating, and explaining as a means of facilitating a substantive understanding of subject matter. The following are suggestions on how to structure tasks to encourage critical thinking.

• **Challenges and problems.** McBride and Cleland (1998) suggest that critical thinking can be facilitated by presenting students with problems or challenges in which they have prerequisite knowledge but are challenged to use this knowledge in new ways. For example, students might be challenged to design an "obstacle course that promotes aerobic endurance, flexibility, muscular endurance, agility, and balance (i.e., health-related and skill-related fitness components)" (p. 45). Students evaluate their solutions based on established criteria for success and then defend or explain their solutions to other students and the teacher. The following are other challenges that could be used to encourage critical thinking:

1. In a sport education unit, scout opponents and develop a winning strategy.

2. In a sport education unit, create a Web site for your assigned team.

3. Analyze your fitness levels and design and evaluate a personal fitness program.

4. With a partner, use videotape or digital technology to record, analyze, evaluate, and give each other feedback on skills.

5. Create a dance or gymnastics routine, record the performance, and conduct a self-evaluation to be presented to class.

6. Conduct a self-analysis of your nutrition habits and evaluate how healthy your diet is. Now, establish a new diet and keep a journal of your food intake for the next three weeks.

• **Teaching methods.** Various teaching styles can be used to engage students in critical thinking (Blitzer, 1995). Examples of methods that can be used to engage students in critical thinking are presented in the following text.

As described in chapter 2, reciprocal teaching places students in the position to assist one another when learning or performing certain skills. A primary responsibility of students in reciprocal style is evaluating one's partner, which requires students to have content knowledge regarding the skill being taught. Therefore, students need to be taught about things to look for, which are the key elements (critical elements), and the instructional cues that can be used to teach the elements important for performing a skill.

Students are expected to provide feedback to one another as they work together to complete instructional tasks. The student who is the observer would watch his or her partner performing a skill while attending to these elements and then provide feedback designed to reinforce good performance or improve incorrect performance. An important role of the teacher is not only informing students about what to look for when analyzing skill but also how to give feedback so that it is helpful and provided in a positive manner. Thus, there is also a significant social element to reciprocal teaching. The teacher should reinforce concepts regarding positive social interaction and communication as part of this teaching method. An example of a reciprocal task sheet is provided in figure 2.4, pages 40-41.

Indirect instruction requires the students to contribute directly to the skill-learning process. Indirect instruction is designed to engage students cognitively in the process of learning by encouraging students to become actively involved in solving problems in sport and physical education. Guided discovery and problem solving are two methods that have been used to stimulate critical thinking (Mosston & Ashworth, 1994).

1. **Guided discovery.** In guided discovery, the objective is typically a concept or idea that the teacher would like the students to discover. So, instead of simply telling the student, the teacher has a cognitive goal and uses a series of questions to force students to think. The questions are

constructed so that students will provide correct responses and thus be guided toward the idea or concept that is to be discovered. When they don't answer questions correctly, the teacher needs to be prepared to ask follow-up questions that will get the students back on track. Students achieve the cognitive understanding that the teacher planned for them to discover, but students had a major role in getting there.

2. **Problem solving.** Problem solving is the reverse of guided discovery. In guided discovery there is a single idea or concept that the teacher leads students to discover through careful questioning. In problem solving there can be many answers, and the purpose of the method is to foster creativity and student exploration of many alternative solutions. The teacher poses problems that can have many possible answers, and the students propose solutions. The teacher's role is to carefully pose problems designed to evoke creative responses. The teacher can suggest solutions when students have difficulty proposing solutions, but the teacher doesn't solve the problem for them.

Problem solving should not be perceived as a way for the teacher to let students do anything they want. There are still lesson objectives, and the teacher anticipates that students will propose reasonable and thoughtful solutions to movement problems. The goal is to have students think critically in order to solve problems and accomplish the lesson objectives. Several examples of problem-solving challenges are presented in figure 4.3.

Examples of Problem Solving

1. In a sport education class, create a scouting form to assess opponents' strengths and weaknesses.
2. Create a 5-minute freestyle routine in gymnastics that incorporates music and at least eight movements that were taught in class.
3. Design a scientifically based personal fitness program that incorporates cardiorespiratory fitness, flexibility, and strength development.
4. Have your partner assume the referee's position in wrestling. Now, thinking of the concepts of base of support and center of gravity, create at least five ways that you can break your partner down or turn your partner over while he or she provides maximal resistance without moving.
5. Design five running and five pass plays that you will use in your offensive scheme for your five-person football team. Remember, all players must rotate to all positions in your offensive scheme.
6. In baseball hitting, have your partner pitch the ball to you. Your task is to discover how to hit the ball to center field, right field, and left field and to hit grounders, line drives, and fly balls. After 20 minutes of practice, I will ask you how you solved these problems, so be thinking!

Figure 4.3   Examples of problem solving.

The teaching behaviors associated with direct instruction are based on Gagne's (1970) learning theory. Gagne conceptualized teaching as the active support of internal learning operations such as motivation, attention, encoding, retention, retrieval, transfer, and interpretation of feedback. Presented in table 4.2 are eight teaching behaviors that could be employed to promote student use of these processes.

Table 4.2   Direct Instruction Behaviors Supporting Internal Learning Operations

Internal learning operations	Direct teaching behaviors
Activating motivation	Use incentives or competence or mastery motivation.
Understanding performance expectations	Provide lesson objectives as advanced organizers.
Using selective attention	Alert students to critical elements of task performance.
Using prior knowledge to assist organization of new skills	Identify relevant prerequisites and prior knowledge.
Encoding new knowledge or skills	Provide verbal (cues, directions) or visual (pictures, diagrams, graphs) input to improve verbal and visual encoding of information.
Retaining	Indicate the structure or organization of subject matter using categories, labels, and the like.
Transferring	Provide varied practice conditions in a variety of contexts.
Using feedback	Elicit performance to obtain evidence of skill attainment and feedback.

Learning Activity 4.3

Describe other ways that teachers can design instructional tasks to stimulate critical thinking. Read the critical thinking theme issue in the *Journal of Physical Education, Recreation & Dance*, August 1995, pages 22 to 52.

Provide Students With Direct Instruction on Thinking Skills

Although students' thinking is related to achievement, many students do not spontaneously engage in the use of effective cognitive-processing strategies or transfer effective thinking skills to other settings (Beyer, 2001; Nickerson, 1989). Often, direct instruction is needed in order to facilitate students' use of effective cognitive-processing strategies.

Weinstein and Mayer (1986; Mayer, 2001) have developed a useful framework for conceptualizing the teaching of learning strategies. The system has five basic types of learning strategies: rehearsal strategies, elaboration strategies, organizational strategies, comprehension-monitoring strategies, and affective strategies. Each type of learning strategy has methods that learners can use to influence one or more aspects of the encoding process. The ultimate goal for any of these methods is to enhance learning outcomes and performance.

Rehearsal Strategies

An example of a rehearsal strategy might be to correctly repeat the steps in a dance. This could be done both physically and with the use of visualization of the dance steps. For beginners, much of the content that is learned early in units is declarative or factual. Students need to simply remember the information. Rehearsal strategies could also include writing or copying material presented in a lesson in a personal journal, answering questions out loud, or telling fellow students what was covered in class.

Elaboration Strategies

Elaboration involves making the material that is to be learned more meaningful. Elaboration strategies would include using visual imagery to remember the skill sequence of a football play or relating a motor skill and its major purpose in written or spoken form. For example, the teacher might ask students to describe the purpose of dribbling in soccer. Other elaborations include creating analogies, summarizing, and using prior knowledge to build bridges between what the learner already knows and what is being learned. Applying a principle or strategy to a new situation, summarizing the key ideas of a lesson, relating ideas that apply to different activities (i.e., the crossover dribble is used in field hockey, basketball, and soccer), and linking content from early lessons to content of later lessons are all elaborations. It is important to note that regardless of the strategy, an effective elaboration will actively involve students in cognitively processing subject matter (Harris & Pressley, 1991).

Organizational Strategies

Organizational strategies are used to transform information to make it more understandable. Examples of organizational strategies include grouping sports as aerobic or anaerobic, organizing motor skills by their taxonomic category (e.g., offensive or defensive or traveling, manipulative, stability), listing movement vocabulary words by their categories (e.g., spatial awareness, effort awareness, body awareness), and drawing or graphing an outline of the knowledge, skills, and fitness required for playing offense or defense in a particular sport. Organizational strategies organize information using an existing or newly created representational scheme.

Comprehension-Monitoring Strategies

Metacognition refers to a person's insight into his or her own cognitive processes and the ability to exert control over these processes (Wittrock, 1986; 1991). Comprehension monitoring is the metacognitive process of establishing goals, determining whether goals are met, and selecting or modifying strategies to enhance the achievement of goals. Comprehension monitoring requires students to know about how they learn. For example, where and when do they learn best? What types of sports or skills are easier or more difficult for them to learn? What are their strengths and weaknesses in terms of skill performance and fitness? As mentioned in chapter 1, learners also need to know about the nature of the task they are about to perform and the expected outcomes. It is difficult to accomplish a goal if learners don't know what the goal is.

Determining whether goals are achieved is an important aspect of comprehension monitoring, and questioning oneself is a basic method of completing this task. For example, if a student tries to apply a kinesiological concept to a new skill, he or she could create questions and write them in a journal in order to answer them sometime later as a retention aid, write a review of the practice session in the journal, or attempt to teach the principle to someone else.

Comprehension monitoring is related to the selection and use of other strategies. For example, accessing relevant prior knowledge not only can help in understanding new material, but it can also be used to check the accuracy of the new knowledge.

Affective Strategies

Affective strategies can help create a climate in which effective learning can take place. Landers, Maxwell, Butler, and Fagen (2001) suggest four strategies gleaned from sport psychology research that can be used to create positive climates in physical education settings: goal setting, self-talk, relaxation techniques, and imagery.

- **Goal setting.** Goal setting is defined as attaining a specific standard of performance on a task, usually within a specified time limit. In sport and physical education, students can be taught to establish goals and hold themselves accountable for achieving goals. Goal setting is commonly used for enhancing motivation and, hence, the climate in a variety of settings. A goal-setting program can be implemented with individuals, groups, or teams, and it often includes guidelines (Gould, 1998). First, goals should be positive, realistic, and achievable. It does no good to set goals that are too difficult to achieve. Second, goals should be measurable based on the students' own past performance. In this way, students can focus on exceeding their own levels of performance rather than winning a game or match. This makes goal achievement dependent on the learner rather than on things outside of the learner's control, such as the expertise of an opponent. Third, the goals should incorporate both short- and long-term components. This provides intermediate goals or benchmarks that permit the learner to gauge progress toward the final goal. Of course, experiencing success along the way will assist the learner in persisting, even when he or she has occasional failures. Finally, target dates should be established and records kept of goals that are attained.

Having learners incorporate goal setting into physical education and sport permits the learners to record progress and helps them persist in attaining the desired performance.

- **Self-talk.** Self-talk is intrapersonal communication or communication that a person has with himself or herself, either silently or aloud. Self-talk involves internal dialogues, instructions, encouragement, and interpretation of feelings. Often negative self-talk will occur when learning or performing skills, and these negative thoughts can distract the student from the task at hand and ultimately disrupt the learning or performance process. The first step in using self-talk positively is to stop the negative self-talk. Students can be taught to recognize when they are becoming negative in their thinking and to use a cue word, such as *stop,* to end the negative thoughts. After negative thoughts have been controlled, counterstrategies, such as positive self-talk regarding past successes, are used. The positive self-talk is designed to displace negative thoughts and prevent the students from carrying negative thoughts into the next frame in bowling, the next game of tennis, or the next swing of a bat.

- **Relaxation.** Relaxation can be addressed through techniques such as meditation and progressive muscular relaxation (Williams & Harris, 1998). Meditation techniques involve repeating a mantra or cue word while sitting comfortably and passively in a quiet, relaxing environment. Deep, controlled breathing may also be used. The purpose is to reduce arousal levels, avoid distractions, and focus on the task at hand.

- **Progressive muscular relaxation.** This consists of having students maximally tense muscles in each of six regions (arms, legs, back, chest and abdomen, lower face, and upper face) for 7 seconds. The muscles are then relaxed for approximately 30 seconds. The learner is instructed to focus on relaxing each muscle group after tensing it. Progressive relaxation is often done in a quiet, dark room with soothing background music. The instructor uses a low and calm voice to take the learner through the tension and relaxation cycles.

- **Imagery or visualization.** This is defined as using all of the mind's senses to create or re-create an experience in the mind. To maximize the effectiveness of imagery, it has been suggested that the performers imagine the scene as if viewing it from their own eyes rather than seeing themselves as if watching a movie. Combining imagery with physical practice will promote better performance than imagery or practice alone. Finally, imagery skills are most effective when the performer is relaxed, so using relaxation and imagery together can be effective. For example, a golfer might imagine a ball going in the cup on a putt. However, before putting, she would mentally scan the body for tense areas. If the arms are tense, she would tense and then relax the arms before putting. The golfer imagines the successful putt one more time and then lets the body take over so that she can execute the putt without thinking during the skill performance. Thinking while performing can interfere with the execution of the skill by causing "paralysis through analysis" (Landers et al., 2001, p. 348).

Summary

Engaging students cognitively during sport and physical education can facilitate learning and performance. In this chapter, several strategies for activating cognitive engagement in sport and physical education are presented, including clearly presenting tasks, cueing to stimulate cognitive engagement, questioning, and checking for students' understanding.

Assess Students' Learning as Part of the Task

Instructional tasks are most effective when students are able to witness their own progress during every practice attempt. This dimension of instruction has been called, among other technical terms, *feedback, assessment, formative evaluation,* and *performance criterion* over the past 60 years. It has become axiomatic in the field of education to talk about student learning as observable behavior since Ralph Tyler (1949) began advocating this way of thinking. The essence of this idea is simple: Students' learning is improved when performance is reflected back to the student as a normal component of every instructional activity. To improve, a person must know how well he or she is performing.

Participation in an instructional task ensures neither learning nor improvement. Students must be encouraged to attend to the results of their participation. Knowing how well a student is performing is an essential component of good instructional tasks in sport and physical education settings (Siedentop & Tannehill, 2000). Nevertheless, such information is rarely available to students in the typical physical education setting (Wood, 1996). In most physical education programs, the extent of assessment is to ensure that students attend class, dress for activity, and exhibit a positive attitude toward the class and teacher. Although these behaviors and attributes are fine qualities, they are insufficient for determining whether students have achieved the outcomes of a physical education program. Neither does being present, dressed, and happy result in winning sport performance. These behaviors are unrelated to the actual performances demanded by any instructional activity where learning is the goal.

Improvement is premised on information about performance. Ensuring that this information is available to students as they practice requires that certain elements be present in every instructional task. These include having a clear sense of the outcome or purpose of an instructional task, making this outcome clear to oneself and to students, exhibiting a means for gathering and recording data about performance, and insisting that students summarize information they have acquired about their own performance. Such summaries should be in graphic and written form. When these elements are present in a task, practice will inevitably yield improvement.

Beyond student success, other benefits accrue from including these elements in tasks. When a sense of outcome and supporting data are present, a teacher can clearly communicate expectations to students in terms of performance rather than attitude and behavior. Having concrete statements about expectations also permits physical educators and coaches to explain their programs to school officials, colleagues, and parents. These task components also produce an objective basis for student evaluation and grading. Curricular goals (good sporting behavior, efficient movement, playfulness, and fitness) rather than attendance, dress, and attitude can form the basis of student grades in physical education. In sport settings, these elements are the basis for selection and utilization of players.

Upon completion of this chapter, the teacher should be able to do the following:

1. Clarify the purpose of the task.
2. Make the purpose of a task clear to the students.
3. Have students keep a record of their performance.
4. Summarize the task data.

Clarify the Purpose of the Task

Human beings can focus attention on only one thing at a time. The ability to rapidly shift focus may give the impression of true multiphasic attention, but it is only an illusion. The centuries-old traditions of meditation and other practices for disciplining attention give evidence of the fact that humans can have only one thought at a time. Clarifying the purpose of a task involves answering these questions: Where should students focus their attention as they participate in a task? What should they think about? What information should they attend to? It is the teacher's job to specify this focus for students. This seems like a straightforward concept. Yet teachers are often concerned with many dimensions of student performance.

As described in chapter 1, instructional tasks can be multidimensional, and teachers need to be aware of the types of goals that might be achieved through instructional tasks. The teacher or coach must be clear about what outcome is expected of students on a particular day, in a certain class, during a certain activity. Other outcomes can be emphasized on other days, in different tasks, or even on subsequent attempts at a particular task. Of course, once students have improved at this dimension of the activity, the teacher can specify other outcomes and things for them to think about.

As an example, figure 5.1 shows a task demonstrating possible foci for student attention. Two students pass a soccer ball back and forth. They must be inside a circle while passing or receiving. The task is to pass the ball to a partner and immediately move laterally to the adjacent circle. In this way, the students pass and move repeatedly. An observer, student C, might be part of the task.

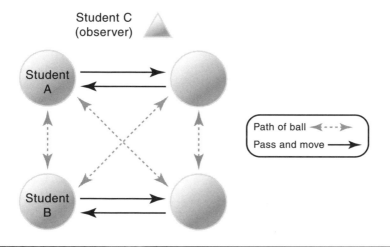

Figure 5.1   Position shift soccer pass task.

What should students think about, or assess, as they perform this task? The answer is "That depends on what is emphasized in this lesson."

- **Movement performance.** A teacher might ask students to focus on the foot contacting the ball. Specifically, the students might be told to use the instep or outside of the foot as they complete the passes. The observer might be told to inform performers about the exact part of the foot that contacted the ball for each pass as the task continues. Or perhaps the teacher wants to be sure that students look directly at the ball as they pass it. Students might say, "I see ball," or "Pass," as they contact it.

    Counting the number of successful passes performed while using the inside or outside of the foot in a set amount of time might be an alternative. *Successful* needs to be defined in this case. A successful pass might be one in which the partner can receive it without leaving the circle. Students might be asked to pass as many consecutive times as possible without missing a pass (again, within the receiving circle and using the instep or outside of the foot). The point is that it is possible to maintain the focus in different iterations of the task. The focus is on correct form and accuracy. When a pass is accomplished using the instep and can be received by the partner while remaining inside the circle, the attempt is successful. Otherwise, it is not. What if a different instructional focus is desired in the same task setting?

- **Activity and fitness.** This involves completing the same passing task with a focus on fitness. Here, students might be expected to gather information about levels of activity, including a task component that requires students to periodically observe and record heart rate during the passing activity. Maybe the focus is on the number of steps (as measured by an accelerometer or pedometer) that the students take while completing this task. Or the focus could be on endurance (how long partners can persist at the task rather than how many attempts they are able to complete).

The point is that students might be focused on fitness rather than skill in completing the task. The elements of the task are unchanged: Students pass and move as before. Yet, the emphasis is now on a different programmatic outcome—fitness. Students are asked to focus on, think about, and gather information about their activity levels rather than movement performance.

The possibilities for task focus are limitless. Most physical education teachers think in terms of a few classic themes, however, emphasizing movement skill, fitness, interpersonal relationships, or knowledge (cognition) in their work with students. Typically, teachers want to focus student attention on one of those themes in any given task. The important curricular concepts in a program are unique to each school and community. What students are asked to think about while involved in instructional tasks should, of course, reflect these local values and expectations. The following is one more example of clarifying the purpose of a task.

- **Social responsibility.** Most teachers are concerned with students' ability to take on responsibilities in group (team) settings. This might become the focus of student attention (and therefore the focus of the assessment) during the passing task. Perhaps students A and B are expected to assess the observer's (student C's) remarks about their performance of the skill. Here, the emphasis might be on the accuracy or completeness of the observer's work. Did this student meet the obligation to provide accurate feedback about performance to classmates during the task? Was the feedback positive and helpful, as opposed to discouraging and frivolous? Did the observer address issues that were noted in the task? Along these lines, all students might be asked to be mindful about responding to opportunities to encourage classmates. Perhaps each student will be asked to give an account of this at the end of the task.

The passing activity is now focused on interpersonal relationships and social and personal responsibility because the teacher requires that students think and gather information about these dimensions during the task.

To summarize, the purpose of a task is not inherent in the activity. It must be specified and clarified. A particular task should be focused on a purpose that reflects the program's mission as well as those things the teacher wishes to emphasize. A different focus can be selected at other times in subsequent lessons. Students must be informed and reminded about the information they are expected to pay attention to. Efficient learning depends on mindful attention to specific outcomes.

An activity that is a regular part of a physical education program is a good place to start. A teacher could emphasize different programmatic themes in that activity. What knowledge might a teacher ask students to be aware of? What interpersonal skills? What fitness parameters? What aspects of movement performance? But teachers need to remember to ask students to focus on only one thing at a time as they are involved in learning and practice. Any of the common themes can be emphasized in any of the regular instructional activities. It is not necessary to change activities when changing curricular focus.

Learning Activity 5.1

Coaches and teachers usually begin thinking about instruction by asking, "What do I want the players to *know*?" Or they might ask, "What do I want the team to *understand*?" and "What should students *learn* today?" Answers to those questions are necessary for preparing to teach. However, if student learning is to occur, additional thought must be give to making the important outcomes (learning, knowing, and understanding) obvious to students and the teacher. You can practice turning vague notions of student achievement into observable behaviors by thinking about the following examples.

When I say, as a coach, that I want players to *know* about proper shot selection in badminton, I must ask myself what behavior would convince me that a player *knows* it. The evidence could be that the player consistently places the shuttlecock away from the opponent's court location; that the player selects a clears shot when the opponent is in the front part of her court; or that the player selects a drop shot when the opponent is in her backcourt. There are many possibilities. The point is that we will rely on actual player behavior to determine whether or not the concept of proper shot selection is *known*.

Now, think about the situation where you want students to *understand* the correct defensive response to different offensive actions in soccer. What behaviors would you focus on? What do you expect to see when an opponent passes the ball? How about when the opponent dribbles? If you said, "I expect players to move up on dribbles and move back on passes," you get the point of this learning activity.

Finally, what do we mean when we say *learn*? When we say that students should *learn* about target heart rate, what things indicate that they have done so? Do we expect that students can identify or compute maximum rate by subtracting their age from a fixed number? Do we expect they can accurately measure their own heart rate and compare it to the target rate? We probably expect all of these behaviors when we say we want students to *learn* about target heart rate.

Make the Purpose of a Task Clear

Helping students understand what is expected is essential to their success in learning. The goal is to reduce learning to an observable, overt action that students can clearly identify. Expert coaches regularly cue athletes on performance elements in novel yet concise ways, as described in the previous chapter. They accomplish this by modifying equipment or the task so that students think about a single element during performance. Further, and to the point, they structure activities to inform students about the quality of their work. Performance is immediately mirrored to the student. The following is an example of how a mirror might work in tennis.

Fundamental to tennis is that players must see the tennis ball in order to strike it successfully. Many errors in striking are the result of students' taking their eyes off the ball too soon during the stroke. This drill ensures that students look at the ball *at the point of contact* with the racket—"look" the ball onto the racket, as they say. There are numerous ways to structure the task of hitting a ground stroke that ensure performers look at the ball at the moment of contact with the racket. Here is one method commonly used (figure 5.2). The teacher loads a ball machine with a few dozen balls and aims it for students to return balls with a ground stroke. To focus attention on seeing the ball at the moment of contact, a dot is placed on half the balls with a felt marker. Half of the balls in the machine are marked with a black dot, and half are not.

Students hits successive tennis balls with the demand that they say, out loud, "Dot," or "No dot" at the *precise instant* the ball contacts the racket. The performance objective is the timing of the student's verbal response in relation to the instant of contact, which is where the student's thoughts should be focused. This might be called a mirror because it

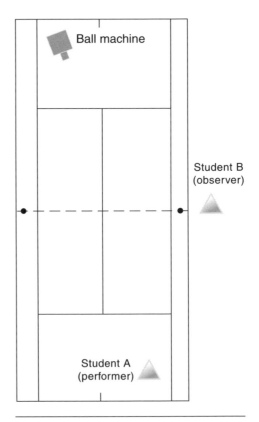

Figure 5.2 "Dot, no dot" tennis attention task.

reflects back to the student immediate knowledge of the performance. If the utterance occurs before the ball hits the racket, then it is clear that the student is anticipating the stroke rather than seeing the ball at the moment of contact. If the verbalization occurs late, it is clear that the student is not really focused on the performance. If the student incorrectly signifies the presence of a dot, it is apparent that she is not watching the ball as it comes across the court.

The point in this example is that the student's visual perception has been made observable. The teacher and the student herself can instantly know whether the performance was "correct." By asking students to report out loud the condition of the ball in correspondence to its contacting the racket, the condition of the student's visual perception is mirrored back to her and to the instructor. The result is achievement of successful visual attention.

In designing effective instructional tasks, the teacher must create mirrors that reflect performance and help students view their own performance as they improve. In the realm of fitness, mirrors are used, such as pulse rate, resting heart rate, time to return to resting rate after activity, steps per day, caloric intake, inches or centimeters of range of motion, number of repetitions achieved, and maximum force exerted. These are concrete, observable indicators for cardiorespiratory capacity, activity level, diet, flexibility, endurance, and strength. Such observable indicators must form a part of instructional tasks when fitness is the concern.

When the concern is personal responsibility and social interaction, mirrors of actual social behavior can be used in clarifying expectations for learning and behavior. Many good suggestions have been offered by Don Hellison (2003) and others (AAHPERD, 2000; Townsend, Mohr, Rairigh, & Bulger, 2003). Students are asked to account for their interactions through the use of journals, interviews, and task sheets. The quality of social responsibility is emphasized through the recording of verbal interactions and rates of engaged time in learning tasks. As a further example, teachers might operationalize leadership (another important outcome of sport and physical education) by observing students' interactions with others, their capacity for setting goals, the degree to which they are logistically prepared for activities, and their awareness of interpersonal climate or the satisfaction of others.

When student understanding and cognition are the goals, the task must include a way to expose their comprehension. For example, strategic knowledge is important in most games. Therefore, instructors want to be sure that students understand a game environment as a tactical problem space. In terms of task design, strategic knowledge must be made overt during activities leading up to game play. For example, when a student is involved in playing an invasion game (e.g., basketball, football, or soccer), a teacher or coach might take the student's first step as indicative of his cognitive perception of *run* versus *pass* (or *dribble* versus *pass*). If the first step is toward an opponent, the student is indicating that he understands the tactical situation to be "run." If he steps away at first, he thinks the opponent intends to pass. The teacher asks the student to be aware of this step and to evaluate it in light of actual strategic developments. If the student's thoughts and decision making are usually wrong, the teacher asks him to consider new and additional information that may be present in the game situation. The point is that cognition in physical education and sport is closely related to choice and implementation of action. (If there is knowledge that is not closely related to action, it is probably not necessary for students to have it.)

Helping learners understand a game environment as a tactical situation facilitates understanding and cognition.

Teachers should answer the following questions when building assessments (mirrors) into tasks:

1. What should students be mindful of as they perform this activity? What should they notice and focus on as they perform?

2. How can that focus on performance be made visible to both the students and the teacher?

3. What action by the students will signify that they understand?

When the purpose of a task is unclear, practice is inefficient and learning results from good fortune rather than the teacher's intentions.

Learning Activity 5.2

The point of this exercise is to make learning outwardly visible to the learner. Here's a sample description: A teacher wanted to have a better idea of whether or not students were contacting tennis balls with the *sweet spot* of the racket face. He was also very concerned that students learn the feeling of contacting the ball in this way. Here is how he changed the environment to make this important concept visible to himself and students. He had a set of three rackets strung with variously sized holes in the face. That is, strings were omitted from the usual matrix to create openings where the sweet spot otherwise would have been. The three rackets, therefore, had square openings in the middle of their faces, each with progressively smaller holes (the first racket had a 5-inch (13 cm) hole, the second a 4-inch (10 cm) hole, and the third had an opening just slightly larger than the diameter of a tennis ball).

Students were asked to "hit" ground strokes with these rackets with holes, starting with the big-holed racket and changing to a smaller-holed racket as their performances improved. You can see that success; in this case, it was swinging at the ball and having it pass through the hole without touching any part of the racket. It is immediately clear in this task when a student is successful because the ball passes through the racket unperturbed. A failure is instantly seen, and felt, as contact with some racket part occurs. The sensation of swinging and having the ball pass through the racket is vivid and encouraging to the student. Success in this task provides a powerful, instant report to the student.

The point of this example is that altering the environment can give immediate evaluation to students. Think about how you can enhance the tasks you use so that information is immediately provided to the student about success and failure. Some questions you might ask to get yourself to get started include: What equipment alterations might help students to evaluate their own performance? Can a sound be produced that gives students information? Can objects or equipment leave marks that give feedback (paint, chalk, and the like)? Can targets be made to move or collapse when successfully hit? Is there a way to supplement activity with student vocalization that will make perception visible?

Have Students Keep a Record of Performance

Once the outcomes of instruction are identified and students are focused on monitoring practice results, they should keep records of performance. The job isn't finished until the paperwork is completed. Recording the results of practice is an important part of effective instructional tasks. Two elements in successful activity programs are goal setting and data gathering. When participants keep written records of performance, two important things result: performance improves (or learning occurs) and there is an increased likelihood of continued involvement and participation. That is, motivation is enhanced.

Keeping a record of the learners' performance can result in improvemnt, learning, and continued participation.

Building on the tennis example described previously, an observer of the performer can use a record sheet (figure 5.3) in the "dot, no dot" activity. The sheet would show each trial, noted as either E, L, or C for *early, late,* or *at contact,* respectively, depending on the timing of the performer's vocalization in relation to the ball's contact with the racket. Since there might be three or four dozen balls in the machine, the observer must pay close attention to the performer. The observer might also share her evaluation of each stroke while recording it. The observer would also make note of any incorrect verbalizations. That is, if the performer says, "Dot" where there is not a dot, or vice versa, the observer notes the error.

As the activity progresses, a record is developed that shows performance. The record can be used to reflect improvement. Ultimately, this task sheet becomes a record of that day's performance. The student is responsible for preserving the sheet or, better yet, transcribing it to a permanent database such as a computer spreadsheet file. This permanent record might be completed as an out-of-class responsibility (study hall, library, resource period)

Trial	Anticipation	Attention
1	E	✓
2	E	✓
3	C	✓
4	C	✓
5	L	O
6	L	✓
7	C	✓
8	C	✓
9	E	✓
10	E	✓
11	C	✓

Most common error: _____E, _____L

Number of attention errors (O): _____

Percentage of successful trials: _____

Figure 5.3   Task recording sheet for tennis attention task.

INTEGRATED PHYSICAL EDUCATION; GUIDE FOR ELEMENTARY CLASSROOM TEACHER by L.D. Housner. Copyright 2000 by FITNESS INFORMATION TECHNOLOGY, INC. Reproduced with permission of FITNESS INFORMATION TECHNOLOGY, INC. in the format Textbook via Copyright Clearance Center.

or even as homework. Whatever the means, students must be required to confront the results of their practice.

Here is another example from the realm of fitness: A teacher wants to emphasize cardiorespiratory capacity by having students measure the amount of time it takes for their heart rate to decline from 70% of maximum to resting rate. This is a concept that students can appreciate only if it is developed over multiple sessions, with repeated observations and recordings, in conjunction with an overall programmatic emphasis on fitness.

Students might participate in an activity until their pulse rate is elevated to 70% of maximum. At that point, students will stop the activity and begin timing as they rest. When a student's heart rate returns to resting pulse, she records the time. Perhaps this activity is done twice per week—on Monday and Friday. At the least, a weekly determination of this measure will be accomplished over as long a period of time as might be available. The task sheet allows for recording minutes and seconds from multiple sessions, as is shown in figure 5.4. There is also a column for improvement, which is discussed in the next section.

Date	Start time*	End time*	Time to RP	Improvement†
15 Jan	1:27:30	1:32:05	0:04:35	
18 Jan	1:07:00	1:11:25	0:04:25	0:00:10
24 Jan	2:04:30	2:08:15	0:03:45	0:00:50
27 Jan	1:30:30	1:34:10	0:03:40	0:00:55
1 Feb	1:15:20	1:18:45	0:03:25	0:01:10
4 Feb	1:50:00	1:54:05	0:04:05	0:00:30
8 Feb	2:05:10	2:08:40	0:03:30	0:01:05
11 Feb	1:30:30	1:33:45	0:03:15	0:01:20
15 Feb	1:44:20	1:47:35	0:03:15	0:01:20
21 Feb	1:52:00	1:55:35	0:03:35	0:01:00
25 Feb	1:27:05	1:30:20	0:03:15	0:01:20
29 Feb	2:07:30	2:10:45	0:03:15	0:01:20
4 Mar	1:38:30	1:41:55	0:03:25	0:01:10
9 Mar	1:00:30	1:03:40	0:03:10	0:01:25
15 Mar	1:47:20	1:50:15	0:02:55	0:01:40

* Record the time in the format of hours:minutes:seconds from the beginning of your rest until your heart rate returns to resting pulse.

† Subtract current trial from original time to RP.

Figure 5.4   Return-to-resting-rate task sheet.

Note that this example assumes that resting pulse has already been observed and that a 70% of maximum has been established for each child. These parameters are concepts that have been developed in previous activities. It is assumed that the necessary computation has been completed. Again, the student transcribes to a spreadsheet the results of the return-to-resting activity.

Students now have a record showing personal performance, improvement, and learning. This record has been obtained as an integral part of the task. What remains to be done is for the students to develop an overview of performance across repeated tasks (time). The final step is summarizing the task data.

Learning Activity 5.3

This activity asks you to think about the recording and task sheets that might be used in activities. Generally, data recording sheets used in activities can take three forms: qualitative, quantitative, or question/response. While thinking about an activity that you regularly use, ask what kind of quantitative data might help to inform students about their performance. Would it help their progress to keep track of the number of attempts they make? Or, would it be useful to have students record the percentage of successful practices (e.g., hitting the target)? Certainly you will want students to record weights and repetitions in strength-training sessions.

Qualitative recording can include observations of the form or quality of a movement. For example, a qualitative check sheet for the forward roll might include things like chin to chest, yes or no?; hands on the mat at shoulder width, yes or no?; hands contacting knees in the tuck, yes or no? The point is that the qualitative recording sheet can be used to reinforce mechanical aspects of an activity or movement. You might also use such a sheet to record the location, speed, trajectory, or other aspects of a ball or shuttlecock in court games. It is precisely this kind of information that good coaches collect during practice and competition. They do so in order to share information with performers that will lead to improvement.

Finally, you may want to use task sheets that require factual or anecdotal responses from students. You might ask students to record their feelings about a certain exercise. You can ask them to describe their perception of effort, exertion, or even exhaustion. You might ask students to write down their strategic thoughts about a play. Here, the form of the task sheet is fill-in or short-answer responses.

Some activities may require all three kinds of data. If there is an idea, or principle, that you want students to master, a recording sheet is an effective way to reinforce that idea. Such recording sheets are also a vivid summary of the student's actual performance in class. Students should be asked to retain these sheets as a record of their work and progress in your class.

Summarize the Task Data

A clear statement has been made about expectations for an activity, an observable indicator of that expectation (outcome) has been identified, and students have a record of individual performance on the task. Now, the focus becomes summarizing students' efforts. Students are asked to reduce the data to a figure or a verbal summary that shows what has been accomplished. The two previous examples illustrate this.

The task sheet for the tennis ground stroke can be summarized in multiple ways. First, the students might be asked to identify the principal error for a day's activity. Did a student tend to be early much of the time in calling out the ball condition, or were late trials more frequent? How many total times did the student incorrectly determine the presence of a dot? In what percentage of the day's trials did the vocalization correspond to the exact moment of contact with the ball? Each student should be required to compute each of these summary values and make note of them. For example, in figure 5.3, there is room at the bottom of the task sheet for this purpose.

Understanding will be enhanced when students are asked to compare these summaries across an entire unit of instruction. Did the number of anticipation errors decrease with time and practice? Did attention improve as the semester progressed? Did the rate of correspondence (vocalizing at the moment of contact) increase over time?

Students can answer these questions with a line graph or a bar-chart summary of the spreadsheet data they have collected during the unit. In addition to summary figures, the teacher might ask students to explain trends that are shown in the form of an essay. In this way, teachers, parents, and, most important, students can be assured that progress has been made and that key concepts are understood.

The fitness example, figure 5.4, can be used to further illustrate the contribution of summaries to student understanding and satisfaction. The result of exercise can be understood only across time and supported by data. Telling a student that it takes her body 4 minutes and 30 seconds to return to a resting pulse has little impact on developing the concepts of fitness or the relationship of activity to fitness. However, when students are asked to summarize and explain personal data, taken from a semester-long fitness experience, the concepts are compelling. The relationship of activity to cardiorespiratory endurance is real, personal, and demonstrated by students with the use of the students' own performance data.

Students are asked to chart the trend in return-to-resting data across time (figure 5.5). In other words, did it take progressively less time to return to resting heart rate after exercise as the semester (and the activities) progressed? What percentage of improvement was there? In addition to presenting summary figures, students should provide a written summary about what happened. The summary would address these questions: How would you characterize your endurance as shown by the return-to-resting data? What changes are apparent? Did you improve during the semester? If so, by how much? Do you think you could have shown more improvement? What would you have to do to show greater improvement? How do you plan to maintain and improve your fitness in the future? A written response to these questions virtually ensures student learning. Figure 5.6 is an example of a student's written summary of the data contained in figures 5.4 and 5.5.

The point of this tip is that the weight of reviewing, summarizing, and evaluating the student's work is put on the student. And the student's

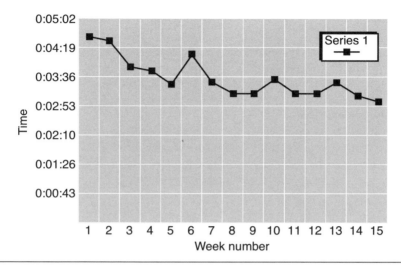

Figure 5.5 An example of return-to-resting task sheet data for improvement in recovery time.

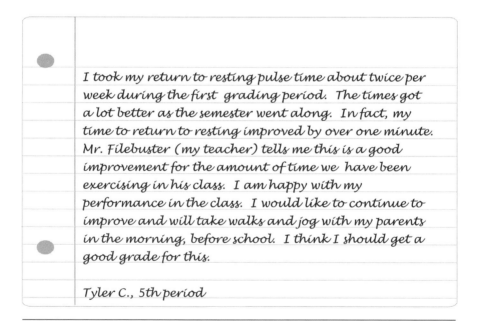

I took my return to resting pulse time about twice per week during the first grading period. The times got a lot better as the semester went along. In fact, my time to return to resting improved by over one minute. Mr. Filebuster (my teacher) tells me this is a good improvement for the amount of time we have been exercising in his class. I am happy with my performance in the class. I would like to continue to improve and will take walks and jog with my parents in the morning, before school. I think I should get a good grade for this.

Tyler C., 5th period

Figure 5.6 An example of a student's written summary of tracking the time to return to resting.

self-assessment is based on actual performance data. Students should be encouraged to share these summaries and data with their parents so that progress, illustrated by unambiguous data about students' actual performance, is readily demonstrated and celebrated.

Learning Activity 5.4

Whenever I ask my doctor what I can do to lose weight, he always gives me the same answer: "Every time you eat something, write it down." In other words, keep a written record, over time, of the thing you are concerned about. In this case, the concern is caloric intake.

Epidemiological studies of exercise and activity have consistently shown that goal setting and record keeping are essential to success and ongoing participation. Keeping a recorded history of performance is a powerful adjunct to learning, understanding, and behavior. The key ideas and skills associated with any sport or movement activity should be reduced to data in the manner we have described in this chapter. An ongoing record of students' progress should be kept by the students. That data should be summarized by students in order to assist their learning and assess their understanding.

Thinking about one of the task recording sheets you developed in the last section of this chapter, make a computer spreadsheet to record that data over time. The spreadsheet can be as simple as a one-column, multiple-row format. The same information from successive occasions will be recorded on successive rows of the sheet.

When students have done this for some time, ask them to employ the graphics function of the spreadsheet to produce a line graph showing performance over time. This gives a picture of student progress and improvement. In this case, the picture can summarize a student's performance for 9 weeks, a semester, or even the entire year.

Further, when students have produced a graph, ask them to provide a written description of the information. Ask students to share these summaries with parents at parent-teacher conferences and during the school's open house. You will find that your program is better understood and supported by parents and colleagues when you develop summary activities as a regular part of your program.

Summary

This chapter has presented ways to augment instructional tasks with elements that allow for immediate and long-term assessment of student performance. We have emphasized the value of self-observation and assessment in learning. When a student is mindful of instructional outcomes, learning is enhanced and made more efficient.

This chapter recommends that teachers who are concerned about improving student performance and understanding should support instructional activities in four ways. First, tasks should include concise statements about purpose in unambiguous terms. This guides student thought and attention during instruction and practice. Second, overt indicators of student focus and performance must be described in the task. Students, peer observers, and the teacher should readily agree about the quality of student performance in terms these performance indicators. In other words, everyone understands and agrees on the purpose of instruction. Third, tasks should require recording these observations. Task recording sheets should be a part of most instructional activities. The recording process further defines instructional purpose and the focus for student attention. An important part of data recording is committing it to long-term storage in a form that is easily retrieved and developed into a synoptic view of a student's performance over time (i.e., improvement). Fourth, students should summarize observational data in both figural and textual forms. When students are asked to be objective about their performance by referring to graphic summaries and by providing written explanations, their involvement in their own learning is ensured. Summaries can be applied to progress in a single practice session, or entire units of instruction can culminate in student summaries of their performance over time (a unit, a semester, or entire year). The emphasis, in any case, is on performance improvement over time. Summaries should include self-evaluation and action plans for future activity and improvement.

These four ideas are suggested as palliatives to the often-superficial and rote involvement that students typically have in their own learning (Good & Brophy, 2002). When students are clear about purpose and objective about progress, learning is the inevitable result.

References

Preface

Chen, A., Darst, P.W., & Pangrazi, R.P. (2001). An examination of situational interest and its sources. *British Journal of Educational Psychology, 71,* 383-400.

Hastie, P., & Martin, E. (2006). *Teaching elementary physical education: Strategies for the classroom teacher.* San Francisco: Pearson, Benjamin Cummings.

Rink, J. (1996). Effective instruction on physical education. In S. Silverman & C. Ennis (Eds.), *Student learning in physical education: Applying research to enhance instruction* (pp. 171-198). Champaign, IL: Human Kinetics.

Tousignant, M., & Siedentop, D. (1983). A qualitative analysis of task structures in required physical education classes. *Journal of Teaching in Physical Education, 3,* 47-57.

Chapter 1

American College of Sports Medicine (ACSM). (2000). *ACSM's guidelines for exercise testing and prescription* (6th ed.). Philadelphia: Lippincott, Williams, and Wilkins.

Bransford, J.D., Vye, N.J., Adams, L.T., & Perfetto, G.A. (1989). Learning skills and the acquisition of knowledge. In A. Lesgold & R. Glaser (Eds.), *Foundations for a psychology of education.* Mahwah, NJ: Lawrence Erlbaum.

Chi, M.T.H. (1981). Knowledge development and memory performance. In M.P. Friedman, J.P. Das, & N. O'Connor (Eds.), *Intelligence and learning* (pp. 221-229). New York: Plenum Press.

Davies, N., & Housner, L.D. (2004). Strategic decision-making: A comparison between novice, intermediate, and expert tennis players. *Applied Research in Coaching and Athletics Annual, 19,* 66-91.

Davis, W.E., & Burton, A.W. (1991). Ecological task analysis: Translating movement behavior theory into practice. *Adapted Physical Activity Quarterly, 8,* 154-177.

Dietz, W.H. (2004). The effects of physical activity on obesity. *Quest, 56,* 1-11.

Fronske, H. (2001). *Teaching cues for sport skills.* Boston: Allyn and Bacon.

Fronske, H., and Wilson, R. (2002). *Teaching cues for basic sport skills for elementary and middle school students.* San Francisco: Benjamin Cummings.

Gallwey, W.T. (1974). *The inner game of tennis.* New York: Random House.

Gentile, A.M. (1972). A working model of skill acquisition with application to teaching. *Quest, 17,* 3-23.

Griffey, D.C., Housner, L.D., & Williams, D. (1986). Coaches' use of nonliteral language: Metaphor as a means of effective teaching. In M. Pieron & G. Graham (Eds.), *Sport physical education pedagogy* (pp. 131-138). Proceedings of the 1984 Olympic Scientific Congress. Champaign, IL: Human Kinetics.

Griffin, L., & Placek, J. (2001). The understanding and development of learners' domain-specific knowledge. *Journal of Teaching in Physical Education, 20,* 299-416. Monograph.

Hellison, D. (2003). Teaching personal and social responsibility. In S. Silverman, & C. Ennis (Eds.), *Student learning in physical education: Applying research to enhance instruction* (2nd ed., pp. 241-254). Champaign, IL: Human Kinetics.

Housner, L.D., & Griffey, D. (1994). Pedagogical content knowledge in motor skill instruction: Wax on, wax off. *Journal of Physical Education, Recreation & Dance, 65,* 63-68.

Hudson, J.L. (1995). Core concepts in kinesiology. *Journal of Physical Education, Recreation & Dance, 66,* 54-60.

Jensen, E. (1998). *Teaching with the brain in mind.* Alexandria, VA: Association for Supervision and Curriculum Development.

Magill, R.A. (2004). *Motor learning and control: Concepts and applications* (7th ed.). New York: McGraw-Hill.

Masser, L. (1993). Critical cues help first-grade students' achievement in handstands and forward rolls. *Journal of Teaching in Physical Education, 12,* 301-312.

McPherson, S. (2000). Expert-novice differences in planning strategies during collegiate singles tennis competition. *Journal of Sport & Exercise Psychology, 22,* 39-63.

National Association for Sport and Physical Education (NASPE). (2004). *Moving into the future: National standards for physical education* (2nd ed.). Reston, VA: AAHPERD.

National Association for Sport and Physical Education (NASPE). (2005). *Physical education for lifelong fitness: The Physical Best teacher's guide.* Champaign, IL: Human Kinetics.

National Association for Sport and Physical Education (NASPE). (2006). *Quality coaches, quality sports: National standards for sport coaches* (2nd ed.). Reston, VA: AAHPERD.

Shulman, L. (1987). Knowledge and teaching: Foundations of the new reform. *Harvard Educational Review, 57,* 1-22.

Slavin, R. (1983). *Cooperative learning.* New York: Longman.

Sprenger, M. (1999). *Learning and memory: The brain in action.* Alexandria, VA: Association for Supervision and Curriculum Development.

Sylwester, R. (1995). *A celebration of neurons: An educator's guide to the human brain.* Alexandria, VA: Association for Supervision and Curriculum Development.

Tanaka, H., Monahan, K.D., & Seals, D.R. (2001). Age-predicted maximal heart rate revisited. *Journal of the American College of Cardiology, 37,* 153-156.

Torbert, M. (1982). *Secrets to success in sport and play: A guide for players of all ages.* Englewood Cliffs, NJ: Prentice Hall.

Ulrich, D.A. (2000). *Test of gross motor development* (2nd ed.). Austin, TX: Pro-Ed.

U.S. Department of Health and Human Services. (1996). *Physical activity and health: A report of the Surgeon General.* Atlanta, Georgia: U.S. Department of Health and Human Services, Public Health Service, CDC, National Center for Chronic Disease Prevention and Health Promotion.

Wolfe, P. (2001). *Brain matters: Translating research into classroom practice.* Alexandria, VA: Association for Supervision and Curriculum Development.

Chapter 2

Beets, M.W., & Pitetti, K.H. (2005). Contribution of physical education and sport to health-related fitness in high school students. *Journal of School Health,* 75, 25-30.

Carson, L. (2000). Fundamental movement skills and concepts. In L.D. Housner (Ed.), *Integrated physical education: A guide for the elementary classroom teacher* (pp. 55-73). Morgantown, WV: Fitness Information Technology.

Doolittle, S. (1995). Teaching net games to low-skilled students: A teaching for understanding approach. *Journal of Physical Education, Recreation & Dance,* 66, 18-24.

Fronske, H. (2001). *Teaching cues for sport skills.* Boston: Allyn and Bacon.

Graham, G. (2001). *Teaching children physical education: Becoming a master teacher.* Champaign, IL: Human Kinetics.

Griffin, J.L., Mitchell, S.A., & Oslin, J.L. (1997). *Teaching sport concepts and skills: A tactical games approach.* Champaign, IL: Human Kinetics.

Hastie, P. (1998). The participation and perceptions of girls within a unit of sport education. *Journal of Teaching in Physical Education,* 17, 157-172.

Hastie, P. (2000). An ecological analysis of a sport education season. *Journal of Teaching in Physical Education,* 19, 355-374.

Hawkins, A. (2000). Educational games and sport. In L.D. Housner (Ed.), *Integrated physical education: A guide for the elementary classroom teacher* (pp. 119-141). Morgantown, WV: Fitness Information Technology.

Herkowicz, J. (1978). Developmental task analysis: The design of movement experiences and evaluation of motor development status. In M. Ridenour (Ed.), *Motor development* (pp. 139-164). Princeton, NJ: Princeton Books.

Holt, N.L., Strean, W.B., & Bengoechea, E.G. (2002). Expanding the teaching games for understanding model: New avenues for future research and practice. *Journal of Teaching in Physical Education,* 21, 162-176.

Langley, D.J., & Woods, A.M. (1997). Developing progressions in motor skills: A systematic approach. *Journal of Physical Education, Recreation & Dance,* 68, 41-45.

Metzler, M. (1990). Teaching in competitive games, not just playin' around. *Journal of Physical Education, Recreation & Dance,* 61, 57-61.

Morris, G.S.D., & Stiehl, J. (1999). *Changing kids' games.* Champaign, IL: Human Kinetics.

Mosston, M., & Ashworth, S. (1994). *Teaching physical education.* New York: MacMillan.

National Association for Sport and Physical Education (NASPE). (2000). *Appropriate practices for elementary school physical education.* Reston, VA: AAHPERD.

National Association for Sport and Physical Education (NASPE). (2001). *Appropriate practices for middle school physical education.* Reston, VA: AAHPERD.

National Association for Sport and Physical Education (NASPE). (2004). *Appropriate practices for high school physical education.* Reston, VA: AAHPERD.

Rink, J. (2002). *Teaching physical education for learning.* New York: WCB/McGraw-Hill.

Siedentop, D. (1994). *Sport education: Quality physical education through positive sport experiences.* Champaign, IL: Human Kinetics.

Silverman, S. (2005). Thinking long term: Physical education's role in movement and mobility. *Quest, 57,* 138-147.

Williams, L.H., & Ayers, S.F. (2000). Teaching "go to the goal" games. *Teaching Elementary Physical Education,* May, 12-14.

Chapter 3

Alderman, B.L., Beighle, A., & Pangrazi, R.P. (2006). Enhancing motivation in physical education. *Journal of Physical Education, Recreation & Dance, 77,* 41-45/51.

Chen, A. (2001). A theoretical conceptualization for motivation research in physical education: An integrated perspective. *Quest, 53,* 35-58.

Chelladurai, P. (2005). *Expert performance in sport.* West Virginia University Distinguished Lecturer Presentation. October, 2005.

Chen, A., Darst, P.W., & Pangrazi, R.P. (2001). An examination of situational interest and its sources. *British Journal of Educational Psychology, 71,* 383-400.

Chen, A., & Ennis, C.D. (2004). Goals, interests, and learning in physical education. *Journal of Educational Research, 97,* 329-338.

Condon, R., & Collier, C.S. (2002). Student choice makes a difference. *Journal of Physical Education, Recreation & Dance, 73,* 26-30.

Darst, P., van der Mars, H., & Cusimano, B.E. (1998). Using novel and challenging introductory activities and fitness routines to emphasize regular activity and fitness objectives in middle school physical education. *Physical Educator, 55,* 199-210.

Goodlad, J. (1984). *A place called school.* New York: McGraw-Hill.

Herkowitz, J. (1978). Developmental task analysis: The design of movement experiences and evaluation of motor development status. In M. Ridenour (Ed.), *Motor development* (pp. 139-164). Princeton, NJ: Princeton Books.

Hidi, S. (1990). Interest and its contribution as a mental resource for learning. *Review of Educational Research, 60,* 549-571.

Hidi, S. (2000). An interest researcher's perspective: The effects of intrinsic and extrinsic factors on motivation. In C. Sansone & J.M. Harackiewicz (Eds.), *Intrinsic and extrinsic motivation: The search for optimal motivation and performance* (pp. 309-339). San Diego: Academic Press.

Housner, L.D. (Ed.). (2000). *Integrated physical education: A guide for the elementary classroom teacher.* Morgantown, WV: Fitness Information Technology.

Housner, L. (2001). Teaching physical education with the brain in mind. *Teaching Elementary Physical Education*, 12(5), 38-40.

Kneer, M.E. (Ed.). (1981). *Basic stuff* (Vols. 1-9). Reston, VA: AAHPERD.

Lawson, H. (1987). Teaching the body of knowledge: The neglected part of physical education. *Journal of Physical Education, Recreation & Dance*, 58, 70-72.

Magill, R.A. (2004). *Motor learning and control: Concepts and applications* (7th ed.). New York: McGraw-Hill.

Magill, R.A., & Hall, K.G. (1990). A review of the contextual interference effect in motor skill acquisition. *Human Movement Science*, 13, 241-289.

McKenzie, T.L., Alcaraz, J., & Sallis, J.F. (1994). Assessing children's liking for activity units in an elementary school physical education curriculum. *Journal of Teaching in Physical Education*, 13, 206-215.

Mitchell, S.A. (1996). Relationships between perceived learning environment and intrinsic motivation in middle school physical education. *Journal of Teaching in Physical Education*, 15, 369-383.

Morgan, K., & Carpenter, P. (2002). Effects of manipulating the motivational climate in physical education lessons. *European Physical Education Review*, 8, 207-229.

Nelson, K., & Cline, V. (1987). Basic stuff in the pool. *Journal of Physical Education, Recreation & Dance*, 58, 32-36.

Placek, J.H. (2003). Interdisciplinary curriculum in physical education: Possibilities and problems. In S. Silverman & C. Ennis (Eds.), *Student learning in physical education: Applying research to enhance instruction* (2nd ed., pp. 255-271). Champaign, IL: Human Kinetics.

Rosengard, P., McKenzie, T., & Short, K. (2000). Sport, play, and active recreation for kids (SPARK). San Diego: San Diego State University.

Solmon, M. (1996). Impact of motivational climate on students' behaviors and perceptions in a physical education setting. *Journal of Educational Psychology*, 88, 731-738.

Sprenger, M. (1999). *Learning and memory: The brain in action*. Alexandria, VA: Association for Supervision and Curriculum Development.

Werner, P.H., & Burton, E.C. (1979). *Learning through movement: Teaching cognitive content through physical activities*. St. Louis: Mosby.

Xiang, P., & Lee, A. (1998). The development of self-perceptions of ability and achievement goals and their relations in physical education. *Research Quarterly for Exercise and Sport*, 69, 231-241.

Chapter 4

Anshel, M.H. (1990). An information processing approach to teaching motor skills. *Journal of Physical Education, Recreation & Dance*, 61, 70-75.

Ayers, S., D'Orso, M., Dietrich, S., Gourvitch, R., Housner, L., Kim, H., Pearson, M., & Pritchard, T. (2005). An examination of skill learning using direct instruction. *The Physical Educator*, 62, 136-144.

Beyer, B. (2001). What research says about teaching thinking skills. In A.L. Costa (Ed.), *Developing minds: A resource book for teaching thinking* (3rd ed., pp. 275-282). Alexandria, VA: Association for Supervision and Curriculum Development.

Blitzer, B. (1995). It's gym class . . . What's there to think about? *Journal of Physical Education, Recreation & Dance, 66,* 44-48.

Doolittle, S. (1995). Teaching net games to low skilled students: A teaching for understanding approach. *Journal of Physical Education, Recreation & Dance, 66,* 18-23.

Doyle, W. (1986). Classroom organization and management. In M.C. Wittrock (Ed.), *Handbook of research on teaching* (3rd ed., pp. 392-441). New York: MacMillan.

Gagne, R. (1970). *The conditions of learning.* New York: Holt, Rinehart & Wilson.

Gallwey, W.T. (1974). *The inner game of tennis.* New York: Random House.

Gentile, A.M. (1972). A working model of skill acquisition with application to teaching. *Quest, 17,* 3-23.

Goodlad, J. (1984). *A place called school.* New York: McGraw-Hill.

Gould, D. (1998). Goal setting for peak performance. In J.M. Williams (Ed.), *Applied sport psychology: Personal growth to peak performance* (pp. 182-196). Mountain View, CA: Mayfield.

Graham, G. (2001). *Teaching children physical education: Becoming a master teacher.* Champaign, IL: Human Kinetics.

Griffey, D.C., Housner, L.D., & Williams D. (1985). Coaches' uses of non-literal language: Metaphor as a means of effective teaching. In M. Peron & G. Graham (Eds.), *Proceedings of the Olympic Scientific Congress,* Eugene, Oregon (pp. 131-137).

Griffin, J.L., Mitchell, S.A., & Oslin, J.L. (1997). *Teaching sport concepts and skills: A tactical games approach.* Champaign, IL: Human Kinetics.

Harris, K.R., & Pressley, M. (1991). The nature of cognitive strategy instruction: Interactive strategy construction. *Exceptional Children, 57,* 392-404.

Housner, L.D. (1984). The role of visual imagery in recall of modeled motoric stimuli. *Journal of Sport Psychology, 6,* 148-158.

Housner, L.D., & Griffey, D. (1994). Pedagogical content knowledge in motor skill instruction: Wax on, wax off. *Journal of Physical Education, Recreation & Dance, 65,* 63-68.

Johnson, R. (1997). Questioning techniques used in teaching. *Journal of Physical Education, Recreation & Dance, 68,* 45-49.

Landers, D.M., Maxwell, W., Butler, J., & Fagen, L. (2001). Developing teaching skills in physical education. In A.L. Costa (Ed.), *Developing minds: A resource book for teaching thinking* (3rd ed., pp. 343-350). Alexandria, VA: Association for Supervision and Curriculum Development.

Magill, R.A. (2004). *Motor learning and control: Concepts and applications* (7th ed.). New York: McGraw-Hill.

Magill, R.A., & Hall, K.G. (1990). A review of the contextual interference effect in motor skill acquisition. *Human Movement Science, 13,* 241-289.

Marzano, R.J., Pickering, D.J., & Pollock, J.E. (2001). *Classroom instruction that works: Research-based strategies for increasing student achievement.* Alexandria, VA: Association for Supervision and Curriculum Development.

Masser, L. (1993). Critical cues help first-grade students' achievement in handstands and forward rolls. *Journal of Teaching in Physical Education, 12,* 301-312.

Mayer, R.E. (2001). What good is educational psychology? The case of cognition and instruction. *Educational Psychologist, 36*, 83-88.

McBride, R. (1995). Critical thinking in physical education. *Journal of Physical Education, Recreation & Dance, 66*, 21-52.

McBride, R., & Cleland, F. (1998). Critical thinking in physical education . . . an idea whose time has come! *Journal of Physical Education, Recreation & Dance, 69*, 42-46/52.

McCullagh, P. (1994). Modeling: Learning, developmental, and social psychological considerations. In R. Singer (Ed.), *Handbook of research on sport psychology*. New York: MacMillan.

Mosston, M., & Ashworth, S. (1994). *Teaching physical education*. New York: MacMillan.

National Association for Sport and Physical Education (NASPE). (1992). *Outcomes of quality physical education programs*. Reston, VA: AAHPERD.

Nickerson, R. (1989). On improving thinking through instruction. In E.Z. Rothkopf (Ed.), *Review of research in education* (vol. 15, pp. 3-57). Washington, DC: American Educational Research Association.

Paivio, A. (1971). *Imagery and verbal processes*. New York: Holt, Rinehart, and Winston.

Rink, J. (1996). Effective instruction on physical education. In S. Silverman & C. Ennis (Eds.), *Student learning in physical education: Applying research to enhance instruction* (pp. 171-198). Champaign, IL: Human Kinetics.

Rink, J. (2002). *Teaching physical education for learning*. New York: WCB/McGraw-Hill.

Rink, J., & Werner, P. (1989). Qualitative measures of teaching performance scale (QMTPS). In P. Darst, D. Zakrajsek, & V. Mancini (Eds.), *Analyzing physical education and sport instruction* (2nd ed.). Champaign, IL: Human Kinetics.

Rosenshine, B., & Stevens, R. (1986). Teaching functions. In M.C. Wittrock (Ed.), *Handbook of research on teaching* (3rd ed., pp. 376-391). New York: MacMillan.

Scantling, E., McAleese, W.J., Tietjen, L., & Strand, B. (1992). Concept mapping: A link to learning. *Strategies, 6*, 10-12.

Singer, R.N. (1988). Strategies and metastrategies in learning and performance of self-paced athletic skills. *The Sport Psychologist, 2*, 49-68.

Singer, R.N. (1990). Motor learning research: Meaningful for physical educators or a waste of time? *Quest, 42*, 114-125.

Skrinar, G.S., & Hoffman, S.J. (1978). Mechanical guidance of the golf swing: The "Golfer's Groove" as an instructional adjunct. *Research Quarterly, 49*, 335-341.

Solmon, M., & Lee, A. (1992). Cognitive conceptions of teaching and learning motor skills. *Quest, 44*, 57-71.

Steps to success activity series. (1990). Champaign IL: Human Kinetics.

Tishman, S., & Perkins, D.N. (1995). Critical thinking and physical education. *Journal of Physical Education, Recreation & Dance, 66*, 24-30.

Torbert, M. (1982). *Secrets to success in sport and play: A guide for players of all ages*. Englewood Cliffs, NJ: Prentice Hall.

Vickers, J.N. (1990). *Instructional design for teaching physical activities: A knowledge structures approach.* Champaign, IL: Human Kinetics.

Wang, M.C., Haertel, G., & Walberg, H. (1990). What influences learning? A content analysis of review literature. *Journal of Educational Research, 84,* 30-43.

Weinstein, C.E., & Mayer, R.E. (1986). The teaching of learning strategies. In M.C. Wittrock (Ed.), *Handbook of research on teaching* (3rd ed., pp. 315-327). New York: MacMillan.

Weiss, M. (2000). Motivating kids in physical activity. *President's Council on Physical Fitness and Sports Research Digest,* 3 (11), ERIC Document Reproduction Service No. ED470695. Washington, DC: President's Council on Physical Fitness and Sports.

Williams, J.M., & Harris, D.V. (1998). Relaxation and energizing techniques for the regulation of arousal. In J.M. Williams (Ed.), *Applied sport psychology* (pp. 182-196). Mountain View, CA: Mayfield.

Wittrock, M.C. (1986). Students' thought processes. In M.C. Wittrock (Ed.), *Handbook for research on teaching* (3rd ed., pp. 297-314). New York: MacMillan.

Wittrock, M.C. (1991). Generative teaching of comprehension. *The Elementary School Journal, 92,* 169-184.

Yost, M., Strauss, R., & Davis, R. (1976). The effectiveness of the "Golfer's Groove" in improving golfer's scores. *Research Quarterly, 47,* 569-573.

Chapter 5

American Alliance for Health, Physical Education, Recreation and Dance. (2000). *Assessment series: Assessing student responsibility and teamwork.* Reston, VA: AAH-PERD.

Good, T.L., & Brophy, J.E. (2002). *Looking in classrooms* (9th ed.). New York: Allyn & Bacon.

Hellison, D.R. (2003). *Teaching responsibility through physical activity* (2nd ed.). Champaign, IL: Human Kinetics.

Siedentop, D., & Tannehill, D. (2000). *Developing teaching skills in physical education.* Moutain View, CA: Mayfield.

Townsend, J.S., Mohr, D.J., Rairigh, R.M., & Bulger, S.M. (2003). *Assessing student outcomes in sport education.* Reston, VA: AAHPERD.

Tyler, R. (1949). *The curriculum process in education.* Chicago: University of Chicago Press.

Wood, T.M. (1996). Evaluation and testing: The road less traveled. In S. Silverman & C. Ennis (Eds.), *Student learning in physical education: Applying research to enhance instruction* (pp. 199-219). Champaign, IL: Human Kinetics.

Index

Note: The italicized *f* and *t* following pages numbers refer to figures and tables, respectively.

A

academic learning time in physical education (ALT-PE) 29
accuracy, improving 10
Activitygram 17
adjustment of tasks
    description of 44-45
    intratask variation 45
    teaching by invitation 45-46
aerobic fitness and FITT guidelines 18-19
affective strategies 100-102
assessment of learning as part of task
    assessment, importance of 105
    clarifying purpose of task 106-109, 107*f*
    improvement and performance 105-106
    instructional task, elements 105-120
    learning activities 5.1-5.4 109, 113, 117, 120
    record of performance 113-117
    task data, summarizing 117-120, 119*f*
    task purpose, making it clear 110-116, 110*f*

B

balance, maintaining 8-9
ballistic stretching 20
Barry, Rick 2
BMI (body mass index) 21
BMR (basal metabolic rate) 21-22
body awareness 32, 34
body composition. *See also* BMI; BMR
    definition of 21
    MyPyramid 22
    primary assessments of 21
    role of diet and exercise 21-22

C

center of gravity (CG) 8-9
checks for understanding (CFU)
    choral response 91
    getting started 89
    guided practice 91
    homework 92
    questioning 89-90
    students' explanation 92
    techniques 89-92

closed *vs.* open skills 3-4, 4*t*
cognitive engagement in tasks
    contextual interference 94-95
    critical-thinking tasks 95-98, 97*f*, 98*t*
    cue and strategy reminders 94
    learning activity 4.3 98
    tactical tasks 53*t*, 95
content development 35
critical elements of motor skills. *See* motor skills, critical elements
critical-thinking tasks 95-98, 97*f*, 98*t*

D

declarative knowledge 14, 15
direct instruction 76
direct instruction on thinking skills
    affective strategies 100-102
    comprehension-monitoring strategies 100
    elaboration strategies 99
direct instruction on thinking skills *(continued)*
    learning strategies 99-102
    organizational strategies 100
    rehearsal strategies 99
dynamical systems approach and skills 2-3

E

effort awareness 31, 32
emotional safety
    learning activity 3.3 73
    mastery-oriented and performance-oriented climates 72
    TARGET approach 72
    "Enhancing Motivation in Physical Education" (Alderman) 73

F

fitness concepts, reinforcing. *See also* FITT guidelines
    assessing 17
    fitness principles 15
    fitness programming 16
    health-related fitness components and skill instruction 16-17

learning activity 1.3 22
MVPA (moderate to vigorous physical activity) 16
Physical Best program 17-18
principles of overload, progression, and regularity 17
principles of specificity and individuality 17-18
regular exercise 15
training principles for program design 17-18
Fitnessgram 16, 17
FITT guidelines
    aerobic fitness 18-19
    body composition 21-22
    description of 18
    flexibility 20-21
    muscular fitness 19-20
    types of health-related fitness 18-22
flexibility and FITT guidelines 20-21
force
    absorbing 10
    generating 10
form and outcome of skills
    critical elements approach 2
    dynamical systems approach 2-3
    form specific skills 2, 4, 4t
    open vs. closed skills 3-4, 4t
    outcome-specific skills 2, 4, 4t
    skill combinations 4-5

G
games, modifying and teaching
    learning activity 2.3 49
    learning activity 2.4 56
    progressive stages in teaching 50-51
    structure of games 48-49
    Teaching Games for Understanding (TGfU) 51-56, 53t
games instruction, NASPE guidelines 47-48

H
Hellison, Don 111

I
individuality principle 17-18
individualized instruction
    description of 39
    implementing fitness component 39
    task sheet 41-42, 42f-44f
inert knowledge 11
information-processing models
    description of 11-12
    information stored in memory 12
    skill acquisition, processing requirements 12-13
    stages of 11-12
instruction, individualizing. See also individualized instruction

learning activity 2.2 42
reciprocal instruction 39, 40f-41f
task instruction 36-39, 37f-38f
instructional cues, selecting
    description of 25
    kinesthetic/tactile and task structure cues 26-27
    learning activity 1.4 27
    pedagogical content knowledge (PCK) 25
    types of 25-27
    uses for 27
    verbal and visual cues 26
instructional cues for students' thinking
    decision making 86
    description of 81-82
    feedback and next response, interpreting 87
    goal of skill 84
    information-processing theories 82, 83t
    information storage 88
    learning activity 4.2 89
    metacognition 82, 88-89
    motor plan, formulating 86-87
    perception 85
    selective attention 85
    types of 83-84
instructional tasks 1
integration in physical education
    language arts 66-67
    learning activity 3.2 68
    mathematics 65-66
    reasons for using physical education 63-64
    science 64-65
    social studies 67, 68
interception skills 5
intratask variation 45

J
Journal of Physical Education, Recreation & Dance 98

K
kinesiological concepts
    absorbing force 10
    accuracy, improving 10
    balance, maintaining 8-9
    generating force 10
    learning activity 1.2 11
    locomotion 9-10
kinesthetic/tactile cues 26, 83

L
language arts and physical education 66-67
locomotion, efficient 9-10
locomotor and nonmanipulative skills 5

M
manipulative skills 5
manual guidance 26

mathematics and physical education 65-66
mechanical guidance 26
metacognition 12
motor skills, critical elements
    classification for 5, 6t
    identifying and teaching 5-8
    learning activity 1.1 6t, 7
    locomotor and nonmanipulative skills 5
    manipulative skills 5
    nonlocomotor and nonmanipulative skills 5
    selected fundamental motor skills 6-7, 7f-8f
movement concepts
    body awareness 32, 34
    effort awareness 31, 32
    "I Am Learning" curriculum 31, 33t
    in performing task analysis 34, 34f
    spatial awareness 32
    types of awareness 31, 32, 34
muscular fitness and FITT guidelines 19-20
music, inclusion in physical education 68-69
MVPA (moderate to vigorous physical activity) 16
MyPyramid 22

N
NASPE standards
    guidelines for games 47-48
    instructional tasks 1
    physically educated person, definition of 77, 77f-78f
    revised K-12 national standards 27-28
nonlocomotor and nonmanipulative skills 5

O
objective, stating 77-79, 77f-79f
open vs. closed skills 3-4, 4t
outcome-specific (open) skills 2, 4, 4t
overload principle 17

P
Pacer test 17
pedagogical content knowledge (PCK) 25
physical and emotional danger and design tasks
    emotional safety 72
    end ball 70, 70f-71f
    invasion games 70
    safe equipment 69-70
    safe space 70, 70f-71f
    stress and anxiety 69
Physical Best program
    FITT guidelines 18-22
    principles of training 17-18
principles of training
    overload and progression 17
    regularity, specificity, and individuality 17-18
procedural knowledge 14, 15

progression principle 17
projections and carrying skills 5

Q
Qualitative Measures of Teaching Performance Scale (QMTPS), categories 76

R
reception skills 5
record of performance
    importance of 113
    learning activity 5.3 117
    record sheet 114-117, 115f, 116f
regularity principle 17
responsibility and respect. See also skills to be learned, analyzing
    cooperative education model 22
    Hellison's social responsibility model 22, 23f
    personal and social development 22, 23f
    respect for individual differences and similarities 22, 24f, 25
    responsible behaviors 22
    strategies for teaching 22, 24f, 25

S
safe equipment 69-70
safe space 70, 70f-71f
science and physical education 64-65
skills and tasks, clear demonstrations and explanations
    demonstrating how to do skill 80-81
    direct instruction 76
    learning activity 4.1 80
    motivational set, providing 79-80
    Qualitative Measures of Teaching Performance Scale (QMTPS) 76-77
    stating objective 77-79, 77f-79f
skills to be learned, analyzing. See also fitness concepts, reinforcing; responsibility and respect
    combinations 4-5
    critical elements of fundamental skills 5-7, 6t, 7f-8f
    form and outcome 2-5, 4t
    instructional cues, selecting 25-27
    instructional tasks 1
    kinesiological concepts, identifying 8-11
    open vs. closed 3-4, 4t
    thinking skills involved in skill 11-15
skinfold measurements 21
social studies and physical education 67-68
spatial awareness 32
specificity principle 17
sport education (SE)
    description of 56
    features characterizing 56-57
    learning activity 2.5 57
Sports Illustrated for Kids 67

static stretching 20
Steps to Success Activity Series (Human Kinetics) 79
strategic knowledge 14, 15
stretching. *See* flexibility and FITT guidelines

T
tactical thinking
    declarative knowledge 14, 15
    importance of 13, 14
    procedural knowledge 14, 15
    strategic knowledge 14, 15
TARGET approach
    dimensions of 72
    learning activity 3.3 73
task, clarifying purpose
    activity and fitness 108
    description of 106, 108-109
    learning activity 5.1 109
    movement performance 107-108
    social responsibility 108
    types of goals 106-107, 107f
task, making purpose clear
    building assessments (mirrors) into tasks 112
    learning activity 5.2 113
    mirrors of social behavior 111
    mirrors reflecting performance 110-111, 110f
    student, understanding expectations 110
    student understanding and cognition 111-112
task analysis
    description of 30-31, 31f
    learning activity 2.1 35
    movement concepts 31-35, 33t, 34f
    skill progression for kicking and passing 31, 31f
task data, summarizing
    comparing summaries across unit of instruction 118
    computing and recording summary values 115f, 118
    contribution of summaries to understanding 116f, 118
    description of 117
    learning activity 5.4 120
    return-to-resting data 118, 119f
    summarizing students' efforts 117-118
    written summary of data 116f, 118, 119f
task design and cognitive engagement
    categories 75
    checks for understanding (CFU) 89-92
    clear demonstrations and explanations 76-81
    cognitive strategies in tasks 93-98
    description of 75
    direct instruction on thinking skills 99-102

instructional cues and information processing 81-89
    questioning to extend students' thinking 92-93
task design (fun, engaging, and safe)
    choice 62-63
    goals or challenges 62
    inherent feedback 62
    integrated tasks 63-68
    interesting content, research 59
    learning activity (3.1, 3.2, 3.3) 61, 68, 73
    music 68-69
    physical and emotional danger, reducing 69-73
    variety, providing 60-62
task instruction
    designing task sheets or cards 38-39
    management of 38
    providing clear information 36
    task method 36
    task sheet 36, 37f-38f
task progressions
    content development 35
    task analysis 30-35, 31f, 33t, 34f
task structure cues 26-27. *See also* instructional cues for students' thinking
task structure for success
    academic learning time in physical education (ALT-PE) 29
    adjusting tasks and skill level 44-46
    designing tasks for success 29
    games and student readiness 47-48
    instruction, individualizing 36-44
    learning activity 2.1 35
    modifying games 48-56
    sport education 56-57
    task progressions 30-35, 31f, 33t, 34f
teaching by invitation 45-46
Teaching Games for Understanding (TGfU)
    game tasks, types 53-54
    model, advocates of 51
    skill development model *vs.* TGfU 54-56
    tactics-before-skills approach, reasons for 51-52
    tactics for invasion games 52, 53, 53t
thinking skills
    active participants in learning 11
    brain development and learning, research 11
    information-processing models 11-13
    tactical thinking 13-15
training principles. *See* principles of training
Tyler, Ralph 105

V
verbal cues 26, 83
visual cues 26, 83
von Laban, Rudolf 66

About the Authors

David C. Griffey, PhD, has been preparing teachers to deliver effective instruction for more than 30 years by developing teacher effectiveness training curricula, consulting with school districts and individual teachers on instructional design and curriculum, and mentoring teachers and coaches. A former editor of the *Journal of Teaching in Physical Education*, he now serves as a reviewer for *Journal of Physical Education, Recreation & Dance; Elementary School Journal; Research Quarterly for Exercise and Sport; Journal of Teaching in Physical Education;* and *Perceptual and Motor Skills.*

Griffey has firsthand experience as a physical education instructor and coach. A member of the Phi Kappa Phi scholastic honorary society, he has conducted research projects focused on effective teaching for more than 25 years. He earned his doctorate in education and psychology from Stanford University in 1980 and received the Blue Key Society's Outstanding Teacher Award in 1990. He is currently director and senior researcher at Center on Teaching in Tucson, Arizona.

Lynn Dale Housner, PhD, has worked with preservice and in-service teachers in the areas of instructional methods and skill acquisition for more than 25 years. A member of the National Association for Sport and Physical Education (NASPE) and the American Educational Research Association, he has chaired NASPE's Curriculum and Instruction Academy and was recently nominated to become president of NASPE. In recognition of his outstanding career, in 2003 he was inducted into the American Academy of Kinesiology and Physical Education, an honorary organization for those who have made significant contributions to the fields of kinesiology and physical education.

Housner is an associate dean and professor of teacher education at West Virginia University. In his free time he enjoys working outdoors, reading thrillers, and traveling.

ENDICOTT COLLEGE

1625 00420 7822

GV
365
.G75
2007

*You'll find
other outstanding
physical education resources at*

www.HumanKinetics.com

In the U.S. call

1-800-747-4457

Australia.............................. 08 8372 0999
Canada 1-800-465-7301
Europe.....................+44 (0) 113 255 5665
New Zealand................... 0064 9 448 1207

 HUMAN KINETICS
The Information Leader in Physical Activity
P.O. Box 5076 • Champaign, IL 61825-5076 USA

Diane M. Halle Library
ENDICOTT COLLEGE
Beverly, MA 01915